HORSES

AND OTHER HEROES

Other books by Don Burt:

Winning with the American Quarter Horse

Winning with Arabian Horses

As the Judge Sees It: Western Division

As the Judge Sees It: Arabian Showing

The Complete Book of Riding

HORSES
AND OTHER HEROES

Recollections and Reflections

of a Life with Horses

Don Burt

The Lyons Press
Guilford, Connecticut
An Imprint of The Globe Pequot Press

The Lyons Press is an imprint of The Globe Pequot Press.

10 9 8 7 6 5 4 3 2 1

Printed in the United States of America

ISBN 1-59228-489-2 (paperback)
ISBN 1-58574-487-5 (hardcover)

Library of Congress Cataloging-in-Publication Data is available on file.

To all the great horses and people who made all of these true stories a major part of my life, and to my writing partner, best friend, and wife, Ardys, who makes sure my scribblings on paper are meaningful.

CONTENTS

Introduction ix

PART ONE ~ Training, Judging, Competition.......1
An Earlier Horse Whisperer 2
Taming the Strawberry Roan 5
Trek to Vienna 9
Two Little Words 16
Communication: A Jimmy Williams Operative Word 20
An Interview with Jimmy Williams 25
Gimmicks: Good or Bad? 29
Nose to Nose, A Different Training Approach 33
Balance Equals Impulsion Plus Collection 36
A Letter from a Fellow Horseman 40
Looking for an Angle 45
The Key to Intelligence 49
Training with the Hackamore 54
The Upper and Inner Mouth 58
From Hand to Mouth 62
Hand Rhythm and Body Weight 66
A Breathtaking Program 70
Judging with 360-Degree Vision 74
The Mad Hatters 78
Riding Lessons 82
At Last! Spectators 87
Making History in the Western Horse World 90

PART TWO ~ Real Hollywood Tales 93
Surprise: First Screen Star Was a Horse! 94
Old Times and Friends 98

Yakima Canutt: A Cowboy at Heart 101
Movie Horses..............105
Greenhorn Horse Traders 108
Jocko: A Stuntman On and Off the Set..............112
Wild Bill Elliott..............115
The Golden Boot 118
Hooray for Hollywood..............121
Boots and Saddles..............124

PART THREE ~ Horses and Horsemen 128
Baldy..............129
River Bottom Heyday..............132
M. R. Valdez: A Legend..............135
Ebony Night 139
Jimmy A. Williams: Another Legend..............143
Clyde Kennedy: Numero Uno..............148
Andy Jauregui: A Cowboy's Cowboy..............153
Mac McHugh: Cowboy Artist..............156
Rex Peterson: Trick Horse Trainer..............160

PART FOUR ~ Personal Memories..................164
A Trunk Full of Memories 165
Chief Rojas: Legendary Ground Man 168
Ray York: Gutsy Jockey..............172
The Breakfast Club..............175
Remembering That First Horse 178
Revisiting a Friend's Oklahoma Roots 181
Back in the Old Days 184
Don Quixote..............187
Just Call Me Rusty..............191
Knowledge Gained Should Be Shared 195

INTRODUCTION

Putting this unique collection of columns together made me realize how blessed I have been to have grown up in a great era of the horse industry. From showing as a youth, through my careers in training horses, judging, and working with Hollywood greats, many equine associations and boards, I've gone down the road with the legends of the industry—horses of the past and present, along with true horsemen and horsewomen.

From show ring to racetrack, to stage and screen, from yesterday until today, many things have changed and many methods of horse handling have been refined. I treasure the memories, traditions, and experiences I've had along the way (and hopefully will have for a long time to come).

I've always felt that whether visiting with horse lovers or putting them in written form, horse stories are best when shared with others. I hope you will enjoy some of mine.

~Don Burt

PART I

TRAINING
JUDGING
COMPETITION

An Earlier Horse Whisperer

I have found lately that if you want to kindle a stimulating conversation, just throw out the question, "Have you read the book titled *The Horse Whisperer?*" Opinions have been widely diverse, from "loved it—great book,—it was okay—didn't finish it," to "thought it was about horses, but it was a love story." Then someone usually interjects with, "I know a real horse whisperer." This opens up the subject that there are and have been several horsemen who have employed the methods described in the book in various forms. The first one I met called it "connecting with the horse."

In the fall of 1948, I sailed into Pearl Harbor on a U.S. Navy destroyer. On liberty, the first place I gravitated to was a tack shop where I met a young polo-playing veterinarian named Billy Linfoot. He was headed for the Parker Ranch on the Big Island to cull some horses, but while in Waikiki, he put on a demonstration of taming and riding a heretofore never-handled young horse in a period of thirty minutes. I was amazed at what I witnessed. Dr. Linfoot and I became good friends, and after my hitch in the Navy our paths crossed often. I accompanied him on vet calls, to the races, and to the Santa Barbara Polo Club. As he was instrumental in the development of the Polo Club, and I stick-and-balled playing ponies for George Oliver (my first client out of the Navy), I was Billy's guest at the Club's opening.

During this time he also traveled around exhibiting his effortless horse-connecting training that took only a half hour. He was a hit everywhere and I was always impressed. It seems that in his days as a student he was quite a daredevil with horses, riding them into hotels and saloons, always wondering how they ticked, and how much he could teach them. As our friendship progressed, he confided to me that he gained most of his knowledge from a book written in the mid-1800s by a Professor D. Magner, who was, at the time, thought of as possibly the finest, most knowledgeable horse trainer of all time.

In explaining his "New System" of educating horses, Magner wrote, "I introduce simple common-sense principles that make the successful control of even the wildest and most vicious horses, not only possible, but easy for anyone of ordinary strength and intelligence to do, which are as humane as they are effective and valuable."

An Eastern newspaper at that time had described this noted trainer as "... a young man hardly of medium size, and of a very modest demeanor. But he is compact of form and muscle, resolute, prompt and decided, though kind and patient in action—requisites more essential in dealing with the many crabbed and cross-grained brutes that are often brought to him to tame, than Herculean strength or size of limb and body." Hardly the description of a man who would use a pine two-by-four to discipline a rank stallion.

As an example, this reporting of a Professor Magner seminar appeared in a Cleveland, Ohio newspaper:

"But the great sensation of the evening," the newspaperman wrote, "was yet to come, for which all were anxious, as many present knew the vicious nature of the beast to be subdued—in fact, there were one or two present who had had good cause to ever remember the great runaway and kicker known as the Malone Horse.

"He is a gray gelding," the report continued, "perhaps 16 hands high, of great beauty and strength, and a will and determination rarely found. The horse was brought into the enclosure, and caused general commentary by his magnificent style and grace of movement. His owner was present, and after looking at the animal for a few moments, and dreading to see him pass into other hands to manage, hesitated at the last moment to give his consent to the application of the system.

"Professor Magner, determined to have a subject for his class, asked the price of the horse, which was announced. 'I'll take him,' said the professor, and at once handed over the amount. This movement on the part of Magner was unexpected, as most horsemen who have visited us generally preferred to 'work up' other people's horses, rather than their own.

"At this stage of the proceedings," the reporter wrote, "the excitement was intense, and many speculations were indulged in as to who would prove the victor, man or horse.

"In less than twenty minutes from the time that Professor Magner laid his hands upon his subject, the horse was as gentle as a lamb, and as easily controlled as the most reliable family horse."

The aforementioned news item appeared in the *Cleveland Leader*, February 1870.

I personally have one of the original copies of Magner's *Horse and Stock Book* and have visited with many world-famous horsemen over the years who actually used Professor Magner's methods.

In fact or as a matter of coincidence, my wife and I were with Rex Peterson on his birthday, New Year's Day, when he told us he had just finished doing the horse stunt work on the Robert Redford film, *The Horse Whisperer*. Naturally, being the trainer of countless movie horses that have rendered scene-stealing performances, his conversation turned to training methods. He said, "Don, it's all here in this old book I've had for years," and handed me Magner's 1887 edition.

Taming the Strawberry Roan

Shortly after I published an article about horse whisperers, I found that my mailbox runneth over and my phone line jammeth up. Some inquiries dealt with the Magner book, namely where to find a copy, but most were about Dr. Bill Linfoot. In fact, one letter was from one of Linfoot's old army buddies, who was also his classmate in veterinary school. After reading the letter, I picked up the phone and called the sender, Dr. Robert Poulson. He shared anecdotes about Billy and his antics but above all, the fact that he highly regarded him as a great horseman. Some of the stories Doc Poulson and I chatted about were from his letter, and I quote:

> "During his college days Bill would ride gaited horses—Tennessee Walkers and jumpers in the afternoon, and bareback and saddle broncs at the rodeo that night. He even married a fellow vet student, Janet McMillan, and what a great pair of vets they made. The entire Linfoot family played polo avidly and the Linfoot name is still sacred around the polo fields. Bill claimed that more of the things he did with horses were learned from his father, Pat, who made a good living buying spoiled, sour racehorses that had been ruled off the track. After about a week, they'd take the horses back to the track and they'd drop their heads and eat grass in front of the grandstand while the band played.
> "Bill was the smoothest promoter you can imagine. About the middle of the month he'd start some rumor and get the barrack in an uproar of debates, starting with one concept and then switching sides. One time he

started a debate over which was the fastest, man or horse, for a hundred yards. On payday he'd have a horse and a man to settle the controversy and a lot of side bets.

"His biggest promotion was a hundred-dollar wager that he could take any horse, and in one hour he would ride it, crawl under its belly, between the hind legs, and even stand on the horses' hocks holding the tail; he'd have this horse following him around like a dog. People used to ask him if they could watch and his reply would be, 'Yeah, for a thousand dollars, but I'd be stealing your money. It would be like watching a surgeon do an operation and that wouldn't mean you could do it.'

"His fame spread and cowboys around Fort Collins were trying to find a bronc to set up this crazy Linfoot. One weekend at a Wyoming ranch where a sizeable crowd had assembled, Bill put on a show I'll never forget. Bill wore too-big bib overalls, one leg tucked in a boot, the other rolled in a cuff almost to the crotch, a fringed square-dancer's shirt, a red bandana round his neck, and a straw hat that came down over his ears. I thought they'd have to get an ambulance to take care of the apoplectic symptoms those spectators were experiencing from laughter. I never saw more tears at a funeral.

"Out behind the barn in a corral was a strawberry roan that must have been the model for Curly Fletcher's poem and song, 'The Strawberry Roan.' He had enough hair on his legs to stuff a double bed mattress and a head that would double the leather cost for a halter. The gleam in those little pig eyes was not one of compassion or for kid-pony candidacy. His brands could have qualified for the preface of the Wyoming Brand Book with his ownership pedigree, but the big number 13 high on his left hip gave a clue to his remuda award. A lot of red showed through his white hair, obviously planted by ropes and spurs, and there was no evidence of farrier technology on his platter-sized cracked hooves.

"Bill dumped out his paraphernalia from a burlap bag and allowed the crowd to watch his preparations and roping the horse—he was quite proud of his accurate hoolihan. As he laid out his 'stuff,' in a voice just loud enough for some to hear, he would ask, 'Didn't we put in the snake oil?'

"Old Roany was sure enough broke to lead. As quick as that rope tightened around his ewe-neck, he came right to Bill at about half throttle. Bill quickly side-stepped. It didn't take long, though, for Bill's horse-connecting to allow him to be perched sidewise on old Roany, who wore a mason-line string halter. Jumping off, Bill began trotting around the pen with that old bronc right at his shoulder, his ears always pointed to his conqueror. The crowd couldn't believe it . . . nor could I, and I'd seen 'it' several times. Of course they wanted to see Bill crawl under the belly, which he obliged.

"Bill freely told the secret of 'how' he accomplished his results, but very subtly, and I doubt many in his audience grasped the 'method.' He was certainly a 'horse whisperer' though he didn't call it that. In fact, he often said it didn't matter what words you used; sometimes he just counted numbers. But he did rely heavily on the soothing and melodious *Whoa.* The main secret was his system of advance and retreat, which Indians and horsemen have used for eons.

"Another 'secret' Bill employed, and a lot of spectators missed, was the use of the chestnut. If you ever saw a Linfoot demo, you would see him reach down and peel off a piece of the chestnut and rub it on his hands and then let the horse smell his hand. It was an old Indian trick in stealing horses, to creep into the enemy horse herd without causing alarm. It is an amazing tool for calming a horse—almost like a tranquilizer—it's plain *magic* to show a foal with its mother's chestnut in your hand."

It's old-time horsemen like Dr. Billy Linfoot who keep the industry alive for a lot of us, so we can share tales as did retired vet, Doc Poulson, who now sculpts bronzes.

Trek to Vienna

The last leg of my recent journey overseas was probably the most memorable, for it brought to reality one of my lifelong dreams: to visit the Spanish Riding School in Vienna, Austria. Ever since I could say horse, which I think was the first word I ever uttered, I've been infatuated with the famous school and its Lipizzaners. All through my youth and adult life I've read about, talked about, and looked at pictures of the classic haute école and now here I was, about to see it for myself.

My wife and I arrived late one evening and, before going to bed, decided to walk to the school. It happens to be right in the heart of town about two blocks from the Opera House. It was a beautiful night, and we strolled along taking in the sights.

We arrived at the building and found something I really didn't care to see: a sign saying the school was closed for a month.

My plans had not included a month's stay in Austria for any reason, so my heart sank. We went back to the hotel trying to decide what to do. Bright and early the next morning, I called the school and asked to speak to Colonel Hans Handler, the director. When he came on the line I explained my plight in detail and pleaded, as one horseman to another, for the opportunity to see the establishment while I was there. He asked me how soon I could come to the school and naturally I said, "I'll be there in ten minutes."

I ran the few blocks in record-breaking time, and I think I rang the bell before he could have sat back down after our conversation.

He greeted me warmly and escorted me on a tour of his offices. He then sent for one of his assistants and told him to show me everything, allowing me to take pictures as we went.

On the way down the long corridor and across the courtyard to the stable, I was given a brief history of the white stallions and the school. There is a wealth of information about the school and the breed—so much, in fact, that it would take several volumes just to outline it all.

The school, as it stands today, was built in 1735. The magnificent riding hall takes your breath away. It is long and narrow, light and airy, and has two galleries and a richly ornamented stucco ceiling from which hang huge chandeliers. Opposite the entrance is a portrait of Emperor Charles VI riding a Lipizzaner stallion. Over the years the hall has been used for everything from housing the Stock Exchange to meetings of Parliament. But since 1894 it has been used solely for the cultivation of classical equestrian art and the training of the white stallions.

We arrived at the "barn," as I called it, just in time to see the first set of horses go out for their work. This set was simply going to the outside riding area for exercise—twelve horses all tacked up, six riders in uniform; ride one and lead one, walk ten minutes, trot ten minutes, and repeat, returning in forty minutes. After the orders were given to the group, they went across the road in formation with me right on their heels.

I'm sure my guide wanted to laugh at me, for my questions were coming at him like machine-gun fire; he patiently answered each one. About twenty-five Lipizzaners are born each year at the school's farm in Piber, Austria. Only those stallions with special aptitudes and proper builds are singled out for the program. The only discipline they know until they are four years old is the halter and basic handling. These horses mature rather slowly but sometimes live into their thirties.

When the training begins, it is limited to forty-five minutes a day. This is to ensure that the horse never leaves the lesson tired or disappointed—a lesson some of our trainers could benefit from. Gradually they learn the basics—walk, trot, and canter—and are physically conditioned before proceeding into actual dressage.

Johann Meixner compiled the training plan for the Spanish Riding School at the end of the last century. The principles, most of which had previously been handed down by word of mouth, were placed in three basic categories: 1.] The forward gaits; 2.] The lower (or campaign) school; 3.] The haute école.

The first basic entails working the horse at the walk, trot, and canter on a long line while the horse's carriage is natural. The second basic deals with the progression where the hind legs are brought further under the body while the hooves are brought closer together, enabling the horse to be ridden into all gaits with collection.

"If," in the words of the riding master, "the maximum degree of haunch bending and body lifting is achieved, and if the horse can perform all the straightforward and complex gaits and raised exercises smoothly and regularly, then he is fit to move on into the level of haute école."

The first two basics have laid this foundation. Sounds familiar, doesn't it? Always make sure the foundation training is well laid before proceeding into the next phase. Simple if you follow it.

Again, to quote: "Every correctly schooled stallion must be a serviceable campaign horse and be obedient to the rider's touch before the difficult is attempted."

Why don't we, at this time, take a young, four-year-old stallion and follow his course from the happy-go-lucky life prior to training, to his performance before royalty? At the beginning of their career, the young horses are put on the lunging rein for six to twelve weeks. This way, they learn to trust their trainer and learn the simplest aids and commands. These horses are broken with great care, for as we said before, they mature late and are not fully-grown until they are seven years old.

For the remainder of the first year they are ridden forward with increasing speed (not running speed but forward motion in all gaits), and are made more familiar with the rider's aids. In the second training year there is a gradual increase in the demands made on him. Flexibility is key, and it is promoted by practicing turns and voltes. Sideways movements, full masses, and frequent changes of gait and pace increase the degree of control and concentration. During this stage of training, the trot is generally preferred, for it gives the rider the greatest opportunity to control the progress of his horse. The "swing" of the back permits him to sit easily and measure the degree of relaxation and the correctness of the hind leg action.

"This work also strengthens the muscles and leads to increased suppleness. This is the preparation for the canter, which encourages the forward urge but, when training, shouldn't be maintained too long because of its tiring effect.

"Riding into and out of corners should be taken with care and thought, making sure the horse always bends inward, maintaining his rhythm and placing the rear hoof exactly in the imprint of the fore hoof." Quite a science, isn't it?

Through this exercise, together with voltes and wide turns bending inward, the horse's body becomes more flexible and his hind legs are brought into play. Much emphasis is placed on the hind legs because they provide the horse's driving force. Alternation of the different gaits and frequent changes of tempo increase his alertness, obedience, and concentration.

The shoulder-in exercise is practiced at a walk, trot, and canter. This provides for the flexibility of the shoulders to improve action and increase the suppleness of the body.

Next comes "the backward step," as they call it, which helps to increase dexterity. Basically, at this stage of training, the stallion of this school is no different than any dressage horse that is showing in competition. The training diverges with the haute école, and its exercises on and above the ground.

The movements on the ground are: gallop; change leads; pirouette (a circular turn in which the horse pivots on one of its hind legs); piaffe (stationary trot); and passage or Spanish walk (high-stepping trot).

The movements above the ground are pesade (a low levade of less than forty-five degrees); levade (in which the horse bends its haunches and stands on its hind legs, raising its forelegs); courbette (hopping on hind legs); croupade (leaving the ground with hind legs bent under); capriole (rising in air with hind legs outthrust). All of these exercises are movements drawn from nature, cultivated by training, and made useful to man. Unnatural movements are despised by the schoolmasters.

The young stallion must demonstrate the ability to learn, while in the basics, before being allowed to proceed into the airs above the ground. The gallop and change of leads is done much the same way our Western horses perform in the reining patterns. The pirouette is a collected canter in a small circle with the inner hind leg acting as a pivot for the forelegs and the outer hind leg—our spinning horses perform modified versions of this.

The piaffe is learned in-hand without a rider. He must be kept trotting but shortened down until he becomes stationary. Then comes the piaffe with the rider, who merely sits quiet and relaxed while the horse, guided from the ground, gets used to the rider's weight while executing the movement.

My guide pointed out that before the horse has the training in-hand for the piaffe, he is placed between the pillars to shorten down. As he said, "It is no good putting the horse between the pillars and trying to compel him to piaffe by using a whip. Plenty of praise and very little punishment provide the only way to succeed."

Not every horse is qualified to learn the pesade, levade, courbette, or capriole. The pesade and levade form a link between the ground exercises and those in the air; both moves are started with the piaffe. In the pesade, the horse's forelegs are lifted off the ground; the levade is the completion of that movement whereby the horse bends his hind legs until his hocks are almost touching the ground, and the whole weight of the body is balanced on the hind legs.

These can either be done in-hand or with a rider but are taught in-hand first, as is nearly everything at the School. The courbette is one of the most difficult maneuvers and it may take years before the breeding program produces a stallion that will have the necessary talent. In the courbette, the horse goes from the piaffe to a pesade and then leaps two to six times forward, without touching the ground with his front legs.

The most impressive movement above the ground is the famous capriole. The stallions indicate their aptitude for this while working on other movements between the pillars—first the piaffe, then the pesade, then the horse leaps into the air and kicks out violently with his hind legs. This demands the maximum degree of concentration and effort. An interesting side note, in this as well as in all above-ground movement: The horse is ridden without stirrups, so horse and rider are in complete balance.

All during the conversation, it was very apparent to me how much emphasis is placed on time and basics; they always go back to the beginning and start their final maneuver from the first basic. When training any horse, there is no substitute for "wet saddle blankets," and here it becomes the steadfast rule; time, time, time, together with patience, is the only way to make a horse that will last. They have no thirty-day wonders here.

Two Little Words

There are two words not commonly related to winning or losing in the horse show ring, and they correlate to the color of ribbons received. The two words are "act" and "react." Winners act, and non-winners react.

Those who consistently take home the blue never seem to get into storms in the arena. They always appear to be at the right place at the right time, are always visible to the judge, and never have trouble in the line. Their horses always stand up for them at halter without a lot of placement. Others that stay covered up, or are hollering "Rail," usually line up at the wrong end and let their horses wander around and gawk. The difference is that one exhibitor acts and the other reacts.

The rider or handler who acts is always on top of a situation before it happens. The reactor adjusts after the error has been committed.

A basic thing like showing at halter is a good example. I've seen people who allow their horses to "let down" all the time outside the ring or at home, and do not demand their horses' full attention at all times. They let them wander, look around, and goof off at home or in the warm-up area, and then they wonder why the horse doesn't set himself up on the first command when it counts. I'm sure it's a mystery to the horse to figure out when he's supposed to be serious and when it doesn't matter how long it takes to stand up properly.

The person who acts has a different approach. Every time he handles the show horse, the animal knows it must give its undivided attention to the handler, whether at home, in the barn, outside an arena, or in the arena. The horse knows he must listen at all

16

times to the handler, who is in complete control. There is no question of whether or not the horse will stand up properly when asked.

On the other hand, there are those who allow their horse to move a couple of steps when mounting at home and then get mad at the horse when it moves off in a class. And there are those who allow their horse to cross-canter on the lungeline and then wonder why it cross-cantered in the arena. And those who allow their horse to nuzzle and nibble, root in the bridle, turn its head, and do all kinds of annoying things when away from the show arena, and then wonder why the horse does the same thing when it enters the ring.

It's like the child who has never been taught manners at home but is expected to behave in front of company. The child will do what he has been allowed to do no matter where he is.

This brings to mind an old fish tale from my first venture out to sea. I was with a real fisherman, one of the best. We got our tackle out and started to bait our hooks. I painstakingly put the bait on the hook so not a trace of metal could be seen. My compadre, in the meantime, had his line in the water a full ten minutes before I was ready. After I finished baiting the hook to my satisfaction and as I held it up, admiring my handiwork, he said, "You sure give those fish a lot of credit for intelligence"—a parallel for those who think the horse knows when he is supposed "to be or not to be" serious just by reading the handler's mind.

A successful show horse must listen to you at all times under all conditions, whether it be at home or in the arena. To have top show horses, you must have the discipline that gets immediate results. To be the kind of person who acts, you must know your horse and his idiosyncrasies and be able to head off at the pass any situation that could give you trouble in the ring.

If you're showing at halter, take the time to observe the other classes, or at least look at the arena for any points of distraction or problem areas such as holes or uneven ground that might interfere with your horse's best presentation. Don't wait to get into difficulty and then have to find a way out. Don't leave anything to chance if you want to win.

In performance classes, the same holds true. Check out the arena ahead of time. Ride in it if you can and read your horse's reactions to things like speakers, banners, and shadows. Relate them to how your horse shows best. Observe the other horses in your class while you're warming up. This way, you'll be aware of anyone having trouble ahead of time so you can avoid that horse or person when the chips are down.

Prepare yourself and your horse by allowing enough time to master the basics, and tune your horse to listen to your every command. Learn to read your horse's personality. Pay attention if he backs off or becomes too aggressive, if he's spooky or tired. Take into consideration your horse's personality traits and how they relate to the surroundings. Learn to act ahead of time if your horse starts to cheat on the rail, fidget in the line-up, or drift while backing up. Correct the problem before it starts, not after it has begun.

Horses are not mechanical robots always reacting the same way every day, at every show, so you can't afford to become one either. Be like the smart jumping horse rider who is so in tune with his horse, he knows that if the horse is thinking about ducking out to the left, it will put its left ear back about three or four strides from the fence. If this happens, the rider has time to drop his left leg in and drive him more to the right, over the jump in the middle, saving what could have been a disaster.

There are instances like that at every show no matter what division you're in. Little details are the ones you must learn to pay attention to.

All who are successful in the horse show business have one common quality—the ability to know in advance how to show a particular horse in a particular class at a particular show in front of a particular judge. To precisely sum it up, the "blues" belong to the ones who act. The reactors divide what's left over!

Communication:
A Jimmy Williams Operative Word

In my frequent visits with Jimmy Williams over the years, he always reminds me that communication is his operative term whether he's talking about a Western horse or a hunter/jumper. Jimmy's philosophy advocates the use of your seat in order to have weight influence, working this along with your hands and legs. The seat should be complimentary to your legs to accelerate your horse, and to your hands to retard your horse. When the seat and hands work simultaneously, the legs aren't working; they are passive. That does not mean they're out away from the horse; they're just not active. When the seat and legs work simultaneously, the hands are passive. This does not mean that the reins have a lot of slack—it means they just don't function; they are not interfering. A horse learns to understand the weight influences of the rider's body. This is what establishes good communication between the rider and the horse. Jimmy calls it "having a conversation with a horse."

Jimmy calls the seat the "mediator" and compares it to an automobile in gear. The seat's the accelerator and works individually with both the hands and the legs. The legs control the hindquarters and ask for impulsion. The hands control the speed and give direction. In Jimmy's words, "Too many riders just ride the front end of the horse. They forget about the motor, which is the hindquarters. Riders forget that the horse has four sides which call for communication."

Posting is an excellent example of how the seat is used to communicate to the horse. When the horse is on the ground, the rider is in the saddle. The horse's hind legs drive the rider back up. In posting, the seat acts as the accelerator and an aid in communicating to the horse. Putting all this together takes some concentration on the part of the rider. It's just a matter of what Jimmy calls, "engaging the brain."

Jimmy insists that anyone who gets on a horse should realize that a rider is always either training or untraining. That is why the mind must not wander; concentration must be in the forefront.

He considers the English saddle an excellent tool in training because it does not have the bulk of a Western saddle. In order to communicate to the horse, the rider must be close to the horse. Even when he schools his Western horses, he uses the English saddle. In dressage, which he has always used, you can't have a lot of leather between you and the horse.

In any type of basic training, Jimmy says, dressage is an absolute must. He knows that a lot of trainers don't like to use dressage, but he contends that the trainers who are successful use dressage without realizing it. Those people who aren't good at this sport don't really use dressage. Dressage doesn't mean drive and pull. It's not about driving with your legs and pulling with your hands. Doing so is like scratching something that doesn't itch, he maintains.

"Dressage, done correctly, is what I call high-class equitation. It offers finesse. The bad dressage rider will have the horse overflexed on the forehand, and not responsive to the leg. I like to say these people are not *dressaging* their horse, but *massaging* their horse," Jimmy says. He advises these riders to get some instruction from a knowledgeable person. As Jimmy points out, the horse is bigger than you. If you can't outsmart the horse, you will get into a fight—and the horse is going to win.

One of the first maneuvers Jimmy teaches a horse is how to make a circle. It is a suppling exercise and one of the best maneuvers a person can teach a horse. The rider should bend the horse around the inside leg. The outside leg will control the quarters to keep the horse in the circle. To do this with a young green horse, he uses the lateral aids on the inside, starting with the inside rein and then using the inside leg.

To quote Jimmy, "If I walked up behind you while you were looking off ahead, and tapped you on the right shoulder, you'd look to the right. The inside leg does much the same, as it draws the horse's attention to the direction you want him to turn. If a fly landed on its side, the horse would reach around and bite at that fly. The leg will just irritate till the horse will want to see what's going on."

Jimmy adds that the minute the horse responds and goes in that direction by following the inside rein, the inside leg should stop the action. The outside leg and the outside rein support the action and help maintain the horse in the circle. These diagonal aids will become more important in executing the circle, as the horse gets further along in training. However, before attempting to circle a horse, it should be bridle-wise and ground-driven.

"Most horses are naturally bent to the left," Jimmy says. "You lead them on the left most of the time and they just seem to bend that way. So, for every one revolution I do to the left, I have the horse do two to the right just to compensate."

Another exercise Jimmy finds helpful is the leg yield. The rider walks the horse along parallel to the rail and uses the right leg to move the horse sideways but still parallel to the fence. It's a forward motion, and yet the horse is moving sideways. He cautioned not to do this for a long stretch. Ten feet would be enough, after which the horse is allowed to go straight.

Another Jimmy witticism: "You ask a lot, you're happy to receive a little, and you reward often." He adds, "If you don't use this formula you'll have an upset horse, and any time you fight out of your weight division, you lose."

Once the horse responds to the leg yield, the next step is the shoulder-in. This forces the horse to drop his croup and rotate his weight from the forehand back onto his haunches, which develops the hindquarters. The front end of the horse is moved off the track to the point where (for a right shoulder-in) the left front and right hind will make one track. The right front will make its own track and the left hind will make its own track.

The rider should maintain the forward motion and keep the proper bend in the horse by using diagonal aids, which would be the right leg and the left rein. This eliminates too much bend in the neck. The left leg and the right rein maintain the forward motion and the proper bend.

Jimmy cautions that the rider should take care that the horse is not bending just the neck, but also the shoulder, so that the whole body is bending. The body must be arched. He says this is the only dressage exercise in which a horse is not looking in the direction it is traveling.

The hands and reins move the forehand of the horse off the track and into the proper position. Once this is obtained, you shouldn't have the horse go farther than fifteen feet. Then go back to a normal forward motion. When the horse is accomplished at doing this at the walk, the rider can do the shoulder-in at the sitting trot.

Jimmy is always careful to not over-train. He does a lot of basic work and rarely jumps his hunters and jumpers at home. His advice to trainers is to be wary of over-training, which allows boredom to set in and creates problems. His rule is that as soon as a horse starts to anticipate moves, it's time to change to a new movement. The trainer must learn when to quit and reward a horse for what he knows.

With all his experience and knowledge, Jimmy says that he is "absolutely still learning." He reads all the books that come out about training, both good and bad, because by evaluating everything he can, he becomes better informed.

An Interview with Jimmy Williams

I had a little one-on-one with my friend Jimmy Williams the other day and all he bragged about was how much his horses love him. I asked him, has there ever been a horse you couldn't get along with?

Oh, there've been a few, some badly abused with that glassy look in their eye . . . but mostly I can waltz around them. Horses have to like you. My horses love me and I want them to love me. I give them tidbits, carrots, and treats; most trainers don't. But that's no excuse for a horse to slobber all over your shirt. They have to stand like gentlemen.

I bribe the grooms to bribe the horses. I can tell when a horse is with the wrong groom, because I don't get the results I should be getting in the ring. It takes longer to get the horse's attention, so I'll change the groom.

Now, I've known Jimmy for a long time and he's always had some kind of special training device that he's dreamed up. So, I asked him if he had any current specialty items he was using in his training?

Well, Don, as a matter of fact, I do. I have an overcheck system. The overcheck comes between the ears the way the Standardbred and Saddlebred people have them, and is hooked to a small bridoon bit by itself. The horse is also bitted with a big hollow German snaffle. The overcheck helps to raise the horse's poll and transfer his balance point from his head and neck toward his hindquarters. The higher the head and neck, the more weight is transferred from the forehand to the hind end.

The result is you get more traction from behind. It's like putting weight in the back of a truck so the rear wheels won't spin in place. Anatomically, 70 percent of their weight is in front of their shoulders and 30 percent is behind. I like my horses' weight to be 40 percent in front and 60 percent behind.

I use this overcheck so I don't have to pound on a horse's behind to get his hind legs up under him. With the overcheck, I ride with my legs and tap him a little with my riding crop, pushing him up into the bridle. The overcheck automatically raises him in front, without a lot of punishment on his hind legs.

Once the horse finds out he balances more comfortably this way, I can throw the overcheck away. He'll carry himself with the reins loose. I never force them. I keep the overcheck loose and I don't leave it on too long.

I knew Jimmy was using a treadmill, and for more than just exercise. Tell me about your treadmill?

It's built like a single-horse trailer, with the floor at about an 8-degree angle. A cord runs through pulleys fastened above the treadmill, and snaps into the rings of the horse's big snaffle to keep his head up if I want to. This way, I can transfer his weight from the forehand to the hindquarters and work him from the rear. It teaches him to walk into the bridle and accept it, which is wonderful for racehorses because they learn to not be afraid of the bridle. They'll push forward and push against their own weight, which is good. After a few times on the treadmill, you'll see these rope reins flopping, because the horses will be carrying themselves in that frame. If you'd been riding them, you'd have had to be using draw reins and all kinds of gimmicks to do what I accomplish on the treadmill.

I've got different speeds on this, starting out slow and gradually speeding it up. You can even have the horse trot. I don't like to use anything that restricts a horse too much, like side reins. I don't like dropped nosebands or anything that forces a horse's mouth closed because it acts like a tourniquet, making the mouth less sensitive. I like them to be able to open their mouths and relax their tongues.

I know when I was training my trick horse, Frosty, I used pressure points to make him do certain movements. Do you use these in your training?

Horses have masses of nerves at certain points on their bodies, and these can be useful to a trainer. I can put my finger on different spots to make the horse turn his head to the left or right. By pressing my left heel about four inches behind the girth and dropping the reins, the horse will look to the left. The same with the right leg.

Behind the root of the tail and in front and in back of the ears there are nerves that, when pressed, will make a horse lower his head. Spoiled horses rear up, putting their weight on their hindquarters. You never see a horse loose and running or trying to escape anything with his head toward the ground. So, with tough horses, I use this nerve system at their poll to teach them to put their head down.

On the other hand, horses are the most ill-built animals in the world and this can cause problems for a trainer. They're really out of proportion. We used to weigh horses on my dad's ranch, weighing the front and back ends separately. In those days it averaged 65 percent in front and 35 percent behind. Dr Willard Ommert says that has changed now. Horses today are deeper through the chest with longer necks weighing in at 70 percent from the shoulders forward and 30 percent in back. The trainer has a tougher job trying to balance such an animal. The longer-necked the horse is, the harder the job will be. You've got to work to lighten up that front end.

Nearing the end of my visit, I asked Jimmy to pinpoint the most important part of training a horse.

I think teaching a horse how to bring his hindquarters up under him and raise his head and neck to balance himself is important. Many people do it backward, knocking horses on their heads to make them lower their heads. That's one of the worst things a trainer can do. You've got to use your legs to get a horse bridling.

A trainer needs to know something about dressage. Basic dressage takes care of all that in any kind of training. I use it in every division, be it Saddlebred, Western, cutting, or jumping. Dressage is the only way to train a horse. Otherwise you're beating it into them and that isn't right. I don't claim to be a saint, but I've always loved my horses. I treat them the same way I'd like to be treated.

Gimmicks: Good or Bad?

Gimmicks, Gimmicks, Gimmicks: One horse trainer says to the other horse trainer, "I just bought the greatest invention in the world."

"Yeah?" said the second trainer. "What does it do?"

"Well," replied the first, "it consists of four straps, one for each leg, and a riggin' that goes around the middle—six different bits, one for each day of the week (we rest on Monday)—a log chain—three strips of elastic—two sawed off shovel handles—and a blindfold."

"Yeah, but what does it do?" asked the second trainer again.

"I don't know yet," replied the first, "but with all that stuff, I should be able to get his attention."

Some horse trainers, or would-be horse trainers, have the impression that the more garbage or junk you can hang on a horse, the more training you'll get done.

Traveling around, I've been introduced to some things that would make your eyes go crossed; equipment that serves no real purpose. When you ask what is to be accomplished from all this, more often than not, there is no answer. There is no actual thought or plan—only that somewhere, the would-be trainers saw somebody with something that looked like what they're trying, and he won everything at that show.

Training horses is a science and not limited to show horses alone. It's not a hit-or-miss proposition, a "thunk them on the head, spur them in the shoulder today, and pet them tomorrow" type of science. It's truly a situation where thought and plan must be the order of the day.

As I've stated many times, all horses are different, as are all riders and, for that matter, all trainers. What works well for one doesn't necessarily guarantee success for everyone who uses that method.

Words like dressage, collection, or flexion are cussed and discussed with very little thought about what is being said, and little knowledge of what the words mean. The word "gimmick" is one of those over-worked, over-used terms. When someone sees a new idea being tried, often the label *gimmick* explodes on the scene. Many so-called gimmicks, however, are useful training aids and have been given a lot of thought before being put into use.

If you have sufficient background and knowledge and are not attempting to make a thirty-day wonder, but have reached the point with a horse where all the basics won't work (and I mean *all* the basics)—then it is time for a decision on a plan. But you must proceed with logic, not with a do-something-even-if-it's-wrong approach.

If you look at the problem squarely, you may come up with a type of equipment, maybe somewhat out of the ordinary, which will work in that given situation—perhaps not in other instances but for this isolated problem.

Where most people get into trouble is with over-use of such devices. They reason, "if a little does some good, a lot should be fantastic"—not so. I truly believe that in the show ring, there are more over-trained horses than under-trained ones. Pitfalls like this are numerous, and knowing when to quit or back off is the secret. People tend to use so-called gimmicks as a shortcut to teaching.

Pressures are put upon trainers by owners who are in a hurry to get in the ribbons. One such owner brought his high-priced, superb-looking two-year-old to a leading trainer. The overly enthusiastic owner paced up and down the shed row while the trainer looked the horse over. After many moments of silence, the owner could stand it no more and finally had to ask, "Well, what can you do with him in thirty days?"

The trainer scratched his chin and walked around the horse a couple more times and said, "I might learn his name."

A lot of truth in that example; but to get back to gimmicks: there are many such devices that do not serve a real purpose, and we see them all the time. A bicycle chain in place of a mouthpiece in a bit, for instance—no way this would ever help a horse. Ropes placed in a manner that would leave a burn, or any compound used to make sores on a horse. Devices like these are sadistic, and no matter how they are used, will not produce results—or I should say, they could produce the wrong results.

Any device used on a horse should actually help his natural way of doing things. Some sound good when described on paper, but when tried—whew! One such gimmick comes to mind: A local engineering student had a jumping horse that would jump a fence or two and stop at the next. This went on for a while and when all the basic methods failed, he decided to design a new piece of equipment. He watched horse after horse and spent quite a time at the drawing board.

His theory was to put a loop in a piece of baling wire, put the loop around the top of the horse's tail, run the other end of the wire up over the rump, under the saddle, and out through the front of the pommel. He'd put a pulley on the pommel so it would slide easily, and then fasten a handle to the end of the wire. Then he would mount the horse and head for a jump. When the horse stopped, he'd pull up on the handle, pulling the wire loop tight under the horse's tail. With this goosing type of encouragement, the horse should jump.

No matter how practical it sounded at the time, what happened when the device was actually used was quite different. The horse jumped two or three fences, and sure enough, he stopped. When the rider pulled on the handle, however, the world came to an end. The loop pulled tight, as planned, but the horse broke in two, bucking wildly. The rider, still hanging on to the handle (as well as anything else he could find) crashed through three corral fences and from there was escorted to the hospital, with broken ribs and a leg all twisted. The best-laid plans . . .

All horse trainers are pseudo-inventors or innovators; in fact, to some it is their stock in trade. They have rooms full of equipment, some beneficial and some not. Some horses seem to stay awake nights thinking up ways not to do what they're supposed to, just as some trainers must stay awake thinking up new methods. It's the cycle. Often it works and at times it doesn't.

What really happens, even when so-called gimmicks are used, is that the particular trainer or knowledgeable amateur spends more time on the horse with the problem. Even though gimmick after gimmick or new thought after new thought is tried, it still boils down to more actual time being spent on the individual horse, and that's what counts, gimmick or no.

What really produces success, after all is tried, sifted, and sorted, are hours of thought and lots of "wet saddle blankets." Yes, the basics still win out.

Nose to Nose,
A Different Training Approach

As the renowned horseman Jimmy Williams always said, "It's what you learn after you know it all that really counts." This is one of my favorite slogans and, with the latest craze (natural horsemanship) to hit the horse industry, I need to pass it along. During the past several years, I've watched this quest for learning blossom into a full-grown search for knowledge. With the increase in clinics and seminars, training, showing, and judging procedures are continually being refined and upgraded.

To keep a secret of the training methods used by some has become passé, as more pros are now willing to discuss and explain their techniques. I have never known a top trainer who didn't pick up tips and ideas that came his way—nobody is born with the knowledge it takes to be a top trainer. However, a good trainer *is* born with the natural aptitude that will lead him in that direction.

Essentially speaking, we've greatly modified the way a horse is gentled and "broke" to ride. Most of our horses now have been under some sort of control since the day they were foaled. Gone are the days when a range horse was run into a corral barefooted and thrown at a run. Then, before he could regain his footing, he was trussed up and given a few minutes to "think things over." When the bronc peeler would jerk the slipknot free and let the horse up on his feet, he'd be pulled to a snubbin' post. If the young horse knew the fundamentals of cow kickin', he'd have one back foot tied up and the breaking would continue. Some horses of that era never did get thoroughly broke. Today, trainers study each horse, his abilities and disposition, and figure out a method that both horse and horseman can accommodate to develop the essential alliance between them.

At our riding club the other day, a clinic was being sponsored. I was not able to attend, but a riding buddy neighbor of mine went and was eager to fill me in on what he had learned. He started with the basic concept that horses are flight animals. This stems from the fact that every meat-eating predator that saw the horse as a food source generally attacked from the topside. The mountain lion straddled him with his front legs to get a mouthful of neck and swung his hindquarters up under the horse's jaw in order to break his neck. The wolf was a leading enemy of the horse, but preyed on him mostly from the ground when the herd was in a weakened condition or vulnerable position.

The clinic's history lesson helped establish how a horse functions and relates to outside influences. This led to the question, "How did man catch the first horse?" I have always figured that more than likely, the horse was caught in a snare that had been placed on a trail near a watering hole. (That's exactly what the clinician told the crowd, so I would have gotten an "A" on that one.)

When I was a kid, I tried to break everything to ride, using all of my imaginable, quixotic notions. I had a steer just about broke to ride when my dad told me not to get too attached to something that might end up on somebody's dinner table. I never could win the battle of gentling the hogs. Their hair was too short to hold on to and their round backs continually kept me off balance no matter where I sat. After a few mouthfuls of dirt and grime, I gave up on them.

My buddy, being in a profession that has been the brunt of many jokes of late, was now becoming a student of the horse. He'd attended numerous clinics—cutting, roping jumping, one where they whip-broke unhandled horses, and another where old methods of sacking out were used. The ones that really impressed him were about simply understanding and knowing how to communicate with the horse.

Then my friend got to the segment of this particular clinic that I wasn't quite sure if I'd really heard about, or perhaps only dreamed of. The clinician told his audience that he had learned from a gypsy that you could actually mesmerize a horse by blowing into his nostrils. He then proceeded to blow into the horse's nostrils, made some guttural sounds, passed a blanket over him several times, and rode him around the corral.

As my neighbor was relating to me how it all was supposed to work, I was having a hard time holding back my chuckles. I asked him if he'd tried it yet himself. He said he hadn't but wanted to. When we got back to the barn I told him he could use a new two-year-old I'd just brought in to try out this new technique. Even though the horse was gentle and already broke to lead, lunge, and ride a little, my friend still wanted to try out this newfangled spell-binding technique he'd witnessed.

We took the colt down to the round pen. My buddy lifted the colt's head up and blew softly into one nostril. The colt sort of got wall-eyed but didn't seem to be under any mesmeric trance. My friend blew into the other nostril and again the colt looked a little funny. I watched his expression for visual signs as I thought to myself, hey, this just might work. They were nose to nose now, my friend blowing gently into the colt's nostrils, the colt visibly ogling my friend, as though captivated. Suddenly the colt took one deep inhale and blew it all out.

My friend made a mad dash for the water trough to wash his face. I haven't tried his method yet. They say you're never too old to learn and, of course, every horse is different . . . maybe he didn't get the right one.

Balance Equals Impulsion
Plus Collection

There's a growing sentiment in the horse show world that says good-moving horses should be the ones to win. Of course, they must also perform the required phases of a given class. But let's do away with the bad-going, cheating, mechanical robots that have been dominating some areas because of whom they have been shown by, and replace them with natural, good-moving horses.

Sounds easy, doesn't it? The hard part is defining a good mover. It's not difficult to see most of the time, but it's tough to describe. Natural, yes; balanced, yes; free-moving, yes; all of these are ingredients—but the horse must have the right combination of all these traits. To be a good mover the horse must be allowed to go naturally, which means without restriction. Don't confuse this with head set or speed.

All show horses must be balanced in order to perform. Balance is the one ingredient that gives a horse that capable, ready look. What makes up balance? Simple—a combination of impulsion and collection. Impulsion is the driving force; all movements are done with forward motion. A horse cannot perform if he's all strung out. He must be driven forward to have impulsion and gathered together to have collection. The hands control the front end and the legs control the rear. Show horses, therefore, are kept between the rider's hands and legs; the hindquarters well under for impulsion and the front end light for collection.

This simply means, in most cases, moving the center of balance to where the horse can achieve a balanced position that enables him to move gracefully. If he's off balance, he will either be too much on the forehand and travel downhill, or he'll be too much the other way, climbing in front and hitching behind. Horses do not all have the same balance point. You have to take the time to experiment by moving the saddle back and forth to find where the balance point is the best and the easiest for him to carry the load. Some horses will never be good movers because of conformation defects, but all horses should be allowed to do their best. Breeders should emphasize good movement as well as other factors when making breeding selections.

Impulsion is directly related to the hindquarters but it starts with the back, which must be strong and straight. Don't fall into the trap of thinking the shorter the back, the better. This can be as much a fault as a too-long back. A back that is too short can hinder extension and flexion of the legs. If the short back is coupled with long legs, the horse usually ends up forging. The loin (the part of the horse that extends from the last rib to the hip) should have short heavy muscles because it furnishes the support needed for the transmission of power from the hind legs.

Many people overlook the hind legs. They are what make the horse go, and how they are used relates to balance. There is a definite correlation of hind leg to front leg. The thigh of the hind leg corresponds to the arm of the front leg. The stifle, gaskin, and hock of the hind leg are counterparts of the elbow, forearm, and knee of the front leg. Because the hind legs are like propellers, there must be good muscling through the thigh, stifle, and gaskin for the horse to move correctly. The length of the gaskin and the forearm should be equal for the horse to have proper balance. Most people fail to realize that the hock joint is the pivot of action. It plays an important role in propulsion. As the feet carrying the body strike the ground, it is at the hock joint that the pressure is centered.

It might be easier to compare the horse's hind legs to our own legs. The hip of the horse is the upper leg of man. The stifle is our kneecap, the hock our ankle joint, and the hoof our toe. What we need to move in balance is, in effect, the same for a horse. When a horse achieves the proper impulsion from behind and the proper collection through the rider's control of the horse's rate of motion, then he has freedom of movement, thus allowing the muscles to flex in an unrestricted manner.

The shoulder is an excellent place to observe good movement. If we restrict the horse too much, the shoulder is not allowed to function at its best and the movements become choppy and hard. If the shoulder has the freedom to work, the legs move more easily, and the concussion of the horse's feet hitting the ground lessens, which results in a smooth, level top line of the back. If you notice the top line on all good movers, whether jumping, pleasure, cutting, or even racehorses, you will see the horse move with balance and grace, maintaining a flat, smooth top line regardless of the gait.

I will not dwell on head position because it is a complete subject of its own. Still, how the head is carried does relate directly to collection. If the horse is to be collected or balanced, the head can neither be up, looking you in the eye, nor dragging on the ground trying to plow a furrow with its nose.

Collection is not just related to the front end or limited to the head and neck. It is the gathering together of all parts of the horse and can be likened to squeezing an open accordion. It is a subtle coordination of movement, not a jerk and spur. You actually draw the horse into a balanced position. Any restriction, either from over-doing or not doing enough, hinders the horse's ability to move properly.

Once the horse's balance point has been established, another essential factor to complete the picture is rider cooperation. How the rider distributes his weight will help or hinder the horse in maintaining its balance. If the rider is continually shifting his weight from in front of the motion to behind the motion, leaning from side to side, taking back on the reins, spurring up and taking back, or looking down at every change of gait, the horse must make adjustments to keep in balance. This will result in the horse's top line softening and he will show duress and resentment. All horses have a point at which they look and move the best. It should be the main job of the rider to know what that point is, how and when to reach it, and how long the horse can maintain it.

Many people have the tendency to try to make all horses look alike, and they happily jump on the bandwagon when each new fad appears. The ones who set the trends do it with a particular horse that, when shown, demonstrates all the good qualities they possess. The copiers take a horse of like substance, but usually with a lesser degree of attributes, and attempt to have it perform with the same success. It may work some of the time, but usually only until the horse figures out a way to cheat, and then a whole new set of problems is born.

Each horse has its own good qualities that must be accentuated and weak qualities that must be dealt with. Both showman and judge must recognize good and bad points. The new direction in showing and judging is to emphasize and reward the natural, good mover. To produce a horse that is a good mover, we cannot reduce him to a mechanical, over-ridden piece of machinery totally created by man to go in unnatural motions.

A Letter from a Fellow Horseman

I'd like to share with you a letter I received from an old friend and fellow horseman, Dwight Stewart. He and I go back a good many years to when we were both training and showing horses in a public operation. Those were the days before specialized breeds or divisions—back when a horse trainer, in order to make a living, had to ride anything he could put a saddle on. The business has changed over the years and I'm not sure, in many instances, for the better. But, I'll comment on that after you read the following:

> Dear Don:
>
> I read your "Feeding Phony Baloney to a Poor Pony" (in *Horse & Rider*) with interest. I'm glad you have nerve enough to call a spade a spade. However, you didn't go far enough.
>
> *The Travesty of the Western Pleasure Horse*
>
> Against my better judgment I recently attended one of our large California horse shows, where I again witnessed debased likenesses of the true pleasure horse. Many of them carried their heads so low that the nose was about at knee height! Their heads were back of the vertical and the horses were back of the bridle. They were being ridden with continuous light jerks on the reins, in a grotesque, ludicrous portrayal. Collection? I wonder.
>
> What has brought on this mutation, this change of form? Why should a pleasure horse travel this way? What are these trainers trying to prove?
>
> We Californios have long been proud of our riders, trainers, horses, and equipment, but today we have become a laughingstock and a burlesque. Truthfully, what else can you call it?

The pleasure horse we see today in the ring, with his head down, ears back, mouth partly open from many jerks, back of the bridle, and with tail flat against his rump, is a poor imitation of the pleasure horse we loved to see in days gone by. That horse was a pleasure to see—with his head up so that his eyes were about the height of his withers, his neck arched at the poll, the head just in front of vertical, and ridden with light contact through the reins. His task was to convince the judge that he had easy gaits. His manners were impeccable. He went from the walk to the lope without trotting, and on an imperceptible cue. He came down from the lope without trotting! He may have been ridden an hour or more before class, but he came into the ring without being subjected to some of the quicker methods of today. He was a thing of beauty and a joy to see.

What makes an exhibitor believe that a judge who has been training, showing, and judging for many years will like a horse with his tail flat against his rump and no movement to it? What makes an exhibitor think he can fool the judge? What has become of the expression "He carries a good tail"?

If today's trainers believe that what they are doing to today's pleasure horse is teaching collection, they need to go back to school. It can only be characterized as a mockery.

There are several definitions for collection. To dispel the idea some hold, collection is not obtained by pulling the horse's head back, causing him to arch his neck. One definition states: "The horse must go forward freely. He must accept the bridle and relax his lower jaw. He must be under control through the reins and by pressure of the rider's legs." Another accepted definition states: "Collection must be obtained by riding the horse forward, toward his head, and not by pulling the horse's head back toward his body."

Ask yourself what you would do if you had an opportunity to choose between two horses on which to take a pleasure ride through the park or across the farm or ranch. Would you choose the horse seen in today's pleasure classes, or the one ridden with light contact, one with a fast walk, a rhythmic trot, and a smooth, flowing lope.

You know the answer!

If today's trainers are trying to make a trick horse— one whose walk, trot, and lope are so slow you must throw your hat down to see if he is moving—some more pleasing things can be taught. To name only a few, how about the collected walk, collected trot, trot in place, shoulder-in, two track, canter in place, canter on three legs, and canter backward. These would be more interesting to watch.

The Western pleasure horse class may well be the most popular Western class if exhibitor interest and participation are used as a measure. A class of forty horses is not unusual. When shows offer senior classes, junior, youth, breed, ladies, novice, green, lightweight, heavyweight, stallions, mares, geldings, Cal-bred, and stake classes, to name a few, the number of entries becomes astronomical!

Why in California, among the finest horses in the world, must we have an imitation pleasure horse class?

Yours truly,
Dwight Stewart

In answer to the above: Unfortunately, most of the gyrations mentioned are not limited to California alone. Nearly everywhere pleasure horses are shown, different mechanical traits show up in different breeds. For instance, I find that there are many more altered tails in the Open, Quarter Horse, Appaloosa, and Paint divisions than there are in the Arabian and Morgan shows. But beware, tail cutters, this is going to change.

There are several new rule proposals just waiting for the ratification time of year, which will either penalize horses with altered tail carriage or eliminate them all together. No one is really fooled because the horse doesn't switch his tail—he still shows his duress in many other ways, as Mr. Stewart brought out: ears back, mouth open, etc., and these traits help separate the happy horse doing the job from the forced robot. It's no wonder they don't look bright and happy; you wouldn't either if you were only ridden at shows and then pounded, jerked, hit over the head, spurred 'round and 'round, and ridden always in constraint and restriction.

About head position: The head should be carried where it allows the horse to go balanced, according to the horse's conformation. All horses cannot carry their heads in the same place because each has a different balance point. This is even more apparent when we look at different breeds. Each one, because of conformation (for example, Quarter Horse vs. Arabian) has a different point of balance and basic movement.

Mr. Stewart's comments on collection are timely. I'm sure some trainers think collection means pulling back on the reins and only retarding the motion. Not so. Collection must begin with impulsion. According to Webster: "Collection is the body formed by gathering."

This means from both ends to the desired amount. Balance is the end result of an equal amount of retarding and impulsion—not just one or the other, but the two working together.

But why, one may question, do the Western pleasure horses of today look so artificial? I think it's because many today don't spend enough time cultivating the horse to move naturally. They copy someone who only thinks of shortcuts. The world is not as it was when Dwight Stewart and I studied under M. R. Valdez and Bill Goodwin, two horsemen who knew the meaning of wet saddle blankets and did not resort to a bag full of tricks. They spent hours just letting the horse learn and encouraging good motion. Most pleasure horses today walk reasonably well—some fast, some slow—but most do show well at the walk. At the jog trot we have a few problems—some are rough, some don't really jog; the mechanics have only made them bend a knee (and not very far either).

But the lope is where we have forsaken good movement when the four-beat (man-made) gait was created. We now have extremes from the overflexed (head on the chest) to throwing the reins away (plowing a furrow with the nose and covering it up with the tail).

How about a natural movement, somewhere between the two extremes, something balanced? The real answer lies with the judges.

If we stopped placing the bad artificial movers and allowed the horses that move free, fluid, and balanced to win, in time (and it would take some time because we would have to develop new pleasure horses), we would be back to the Western pleasure horse once again being a thing of beauty and a pleasure to ride.

Thanks, Dwight, for the letter. You can be sure I'll keep on calling a spade a spade, and that I'll go even deeper as time shuffles the deck.

Looking for an Angle

I've found that certain words have a way of bringing things into perspective. Such is the case at hand. I was listening to a talk at a judge's seminar, and the teacher used the words ideal and optimum to interpret the type and conformation portion of judging. All through the rules we find references and some percentage factors given to these areas. The most weight naturally is given in the halter or in-hand classes, and different criteria is used for the performance division.

The *ideal* or "standard of excellence" for most associations consists of a drawing: Quarter Horse and Appaloosa by Oren Mixer; Arabian by Gladys Brown Edwards; Morgan by Jeanne Mellin Herrick, to name a few. The *ideal* may be the mental image perceived in those classes that resemble the beauty pageants, but other criteria should be adopted in the riding sections. The teacher referred to that as *optimum* and it made a lot of sense. The horse having those traits or characteristics most conducive to the task involved, whether trail horse, cow horse, hunter, etc., would probably not equal the ideal at halter but he'd be *optimum* using the traits necessary for that job.

The optimum English pleasure horse in the Arabian division would likely have the same basic optimum as the costume horse, but not the same optimum as the Western pleasure horse or hunter. He could, however, come close to the ideal at halter using those certain important traits and characteristics.

Then, looking at ideal vs. optimum, the language allows us to use the true percentage factor for type and conformation to a more realistic degree. The trail horse, for instance, could have optimum

45

qualities for that particular class, fitting the trail horse picture, but be somewhat less than the ideal in-hand horse.

This all leads to one of my favorite topics: angulation, which is the end result of each horse's individual capabilities. The teacher related that all horses, whatever their age, have the same basic bone length relationship regardless of breed, but that the angle of the bones is what actually makes the horse work. Shoulder angles when changed affect the neck and back appearance as to length and workability. Angles in the hindquarters (hip, leg, etc.) have the same effect. They change not only the appearance—as seen, for example, in the difference between Arabs to Quarter Horses—but also the workability, as with the shoulder angle. What would be optimum for a racehorse would not be the same standard for a park horse. The angles would be quite different but could correlate to the ideal where breed standards are concerned.

All of this is quite evident within the various breeds. Breeders and judges are picking certain traits (optimums) that relate to jobs, while trying to maintain breed characteristics (ideals). In the Quarter Horse breed, we find the trends quite different from the reining horse to the hunter. Even the pleasure horses have taken on individual optimums, from Western to English. The appearance has changed as far as the bone angles, but breed-type basics have not. In the Arabian division, the same evolutions are taking place. The park horse optimum, Western horse optimum, and hunter style optimum are emerging as three separate kinds of Arabians. You can have optimum traits for a given job without losing the ideal qualities of Arabian type.

Horses are becoming identifiable as English, Western, hunter, etc. All breeds of horses are experiencing similar directional changes. Instead of just breeding horse to horse, hoping for as close to the ideal standard as possible, the breeders of the future are directing their programs toward optimum efficiency for the given job. When this takes place, you can actually tell at a young age the direction the foal will probably take. Bones grow and muscles develop, but the angle correlations don't change. Shoulder, croup, and hip angles stay the same. Length of reach and height of leg or knee (high, low, or reaching action) comes from the shoulder, neck, withers (back) relationship. Power or impulsion up and down and length of stride (hindquarters) are all related to the hip, croup, and hindleg angles. Naturally, these angles are also related to the front or shoulder angles for a complete picture.

"Optimum relates to ideal for the job desired." A quote worth filing in your memory bank for recall every time a horse is viewed in relationship to another.

From the judge's standpoint, using that type of philosophy, halter horses can look like halter horses and hunters can look like hunters while maintaining breed characteristics (type). This could rid us of much confusion. The conformation portion of the open Western rules would have some meaning. The so-called halter horses could then be ridden and the ridden horses could halter, using the "ideal-optimum" method of looking at a horse.

Unfortunately in too many instances, one never relates to the horse's optimum ability when personal desires interfere. When someone wants a halter horse, a park horse, English or Western pleasure, reining, roping, or cow horse, they often look but rarely see! Horses that should be in one performance class or another are forced into the wrong categories simply because the owner wants them to be something other than what their potential dictates.

Breeders or farm managers often select the horses for whatever direction their program is primarily based on, when a simple open-minded inspection would reveal the horse's optimum physical abilities.

When analyzing the front angles (shoulders), it is important to relate directly to the withers (which many overlook). The withers begin shortly after the neck ends. Withers should be well-sloped and covered with muscles at the sides. A horse with good height of wither usually has a long shoulder that slopes and is well laid-back. Withers of good height also provide better suspension.

An upright or straight shoulder limits the horse's freedom of forward action and results in a shorter more upright stride. Horses with short straight shoulders give the appearance of having short necks. In appearance, a horse with a well laid-back shoulder and good withers has a short back. To the contrary, low withers and upright shoulders give the appearance of a long back.

In the rear, relating to most good performance qualities, the quarters tend to be long and level or sloping in order for the line from the point of the hip to the point of the buttock to be long. The angle made by *this* line and the line from the point of the buttock to the stifle joint should be very sharp. Angles in shoulders and quarters determine the horse's action or lack of same and definitely relate to appearance and suitability for a given job, ideal, and optimum.

The Key to Intelligence

It was getting late and I was in a hurry. I grabbed the blanket, walked into the stall, and threw it on the horse. The next thing I knew I was picking myself up after being kicked right out the door. As the hole in my leg was being stitched up, I tried to figure out why a normally calm horse would do a thing like that. I went back and looked at the horse and discovered that what I had done was move in his "blind spot," an area where he couldn't see, and he reacted.

This particular horse was a little Roman-nosed and a bit pig-eyed. This all happened years ago, but it taught me how important it is to evaluate the horse's head. We often look but don't "see."

Everyone can see if the head is pretty or not—some judges are even accused of only looking for a pretty head and nothing else—or if the neck is upside down. However, many have no idea how important the function of the head and neck really are. They actually control what the horse is and, to a great extent, what he can do.

By categorizing these parts, we can break the head into segments: The forehead, which extends from the poll, between the ears, just over and a little under the eyes (covering the brain cavity), should be ample to encase a brain large enough to allow the horse to expand his intelligence capability.

A large nostril allows for adequate air intake, especially under stress conditions. A clean throatlatch and space between the jowls also aids in the horse's breathing process. Small nostrils, on the other hand, are usually associated with short, flat ribs, and, consequently, a chest that lacks capacity.

The eyes should be large, round, expressive, and set wide apart. Where the eyes are placed on the head, as well as their size and shape, is extremely important because it relates to the horse's disposition and basic intelligence. We want eyes that are characterized by clearness, deep coloration, and intensity of reflection. Wall eyes, pop eyes, and pig eyes are undesirable. Eyes that are too small, narrow, or squinty with coarse lids restrict a horse's vision. If they're placed poorly on the head, vision is curtailed even further. This, in turn, has a bearing on actions and reactions, which often become defensive due to lack of sight.

The ears should be small (usually smaller in stallions than in mares), thin, and well-shaped with tips that curve slightly inward. The ears, well set, also will give a clue to disposition. The direction and movement of the ears are indicators of temperament. Ears kept in a constant state of unrest can tip you off to nervousness or even impaired vision. Motionless ears are an indication of a slow, lazy, sluggish disposition. The eyes and ears tell you a lot about the horse at first glance.

The jaws should meet evenly. Protruding or receding lower jaws (monkey mouth or parrot mouth) are undesirable—besides being unsightly, they interfere with good chewing ability. The lower jaw also supports the bit and receives the directions or impulses from the bit.

The head does not stand alone. It is correlated with the neck, and the two working together as a unit will determine much about the horse and how he functions. First, you must observe how the neck comes out of the body. Is it smooth? Does the bottom of the neck come out of the body at the chest floor? If not, is it a third of the way up? Halfway up? Is there a positive stop between the base of the neck and the beginning of the chest?

The neck is an extremely important part of the horse's way of going and is probably less emphasized than any other portion. The neck is the horse's counterbalance, which enables him to transfer his weight from his hind legs to his front legs or front to hind. If the horse happens to be a jumper or hunter, the neck is the first part that arches when he goes to jump a fence. He lifts his neck, which helps him get his weight up off his front end, fold his legs, and drive off his hindquarters. Moving the neck from side to side enables a horse to turn around using his entire body. Obviously, a horse with a short neck is hampered in his attempt to bend because his neck is thick and inflexible, and flexibility is the key to performance.

A horse that has a thick, stiff neck usually pivots his body around his front legs when he's taking a gradual turn; with the pivot point over the foreleg, he then swings his hind legs to the outside of the turn and turns his nose to the inside. Obviously for working horses, the method of turning has been altered to shift the weight to the hindquarters and pivot on the hind legs rather than the front. This is especially true for sharp turns or spins. Even a horse turning around a barrel needs a flexible neck to simply bend around the curve. Otherwise, he would be hampered by a short, thick neck, which would force him to pivot over his front legs.

It is also important to note the amount of "crest" in relation to the age of the horse and the sex. The horse with the thick cresty neck (especially mares and geldings) presents many problems. He is usually obese and is a likely candidate for founder; not generally a horse with a great deal of endurance. He is a horse that, though he may be an easy keeper, would rather spend the day eating and little of his time working. The mare with the thick cresty neck shows evidence of masculinity and often is a difficult breeder. Sometimes crestiness in mares and geldings can be corrected with proper diet, however.

It's important to notice the presence or absence of swelling in the poll and the cleanness of the throatlatch. A deep, thick throatlatch could indicate that a horse has an exceptional amount of fat around his airway, which may not provide him with sufficient air for performance. Likewise, a horse with an exceptionally sharp throatlatch (especially one that has a tendency to overflex) would have a restriction of air from the outside to the lungs.

The neck occupies the area between the poll, withers, shoulder, and breast. In all types of horses it must be of a proportionate length. The length of the neck is an important consideration from a performance standpoint and it does vary with the type of horse. Of course, the most desirable (from a performance standpoint) is the one that is long from the poll to the crest and clean in the throatlatch. This gives the horse the room to flex, give to the bit, and still breathe efficiently.

A ewe-neck shows a depression in front of the withers and is the reverse of what is desirable. It is oftentimes referred to as a neck that is on upside down. Sometimes you'll see a horse that is "lop-necked" or "broken-crested"; where the crest seems to fall over. Then you might find a nice long neck but a thick throatlatch. The neck bulges below the jowl and eludes grace; even though the breathing may not be greatly impaired, the horse will be less supple and less responsive. The slope, size, and condition of the neck together with the appropriate head allows the horse to carry himself in the best position. This "best" position is one that is comfortable and gives the horse the freedom of movement and balance that allows him to demonstrate his athletic ability.

Horses do not all carry their heads in exactly the same place. Horses with naturally high arched necks (especially if they come out of the body a little high) will carry a more vertical head position and require a little more collection to be balanced and go in rhythm. Horses with a naturally lower neck carriage (that flexes more at the withers than at the poll) will carry a lower head and require less in the way of collection to move in balance. The ideal, of course, would be the one in the middle.

Because the neck is so important in the overall performance of the horse, it should be included in the conditioning program and not allowed to lose muscle tone or gain excessive fatty tissue. Just as the neck ties into the withers and the shoulder to blend into the rest of the horse, the eye remains the key to intelligence.

Training with the Hackamore

A cliché heard frequently in modern society is, "What goes around, comes around." How true. In our current two- and three-year-old Western pleasure futurities, as well as in all junior horse classes and national snaffle bit competitions, the common use of the hackamore (bosal) has been reborn.

The word "hackamore" used to be preceded by the name "California," which is where this technique of taming and training colts (with no bit in the mouth) was developed, and attained its highest level of perfection.

If we delve into the history of horsemanship around the world, we soon discover that there are certain similarities of equipment and training methods. Tracing the horse back through time, we find that he was probably first used by man as a means of transportation (or for fighting) in the Indus Valley (India) around the nineteenth century B.C. Slowly his use in serving man spread through the East (China), to the North (Mongolia and Russia), and to the West (Turkey, Persia, Syria, and others).

For leading, tying, and directing the horse, some kind of halter with a noseband, headstall, browband, and a throatlatch had to be invented. This headgear was introduced early—when prehistoric man first approached the horse with the intention of taming him rather than killing him for food.

Even today, Arabian Bedouins of Syria and Arabia still exclusively use a bosal-type contraption made of light chains; the horse is controlled with only one woven wool rein. This kind of halter (used on camels) was known in some Arabian countries as the "hackma." In Tunisia, the word *hackma* designated the full headgear for the horse. In passing to Spain and the Spanish language, it became *jaquima* and later, arriving on the American continent, it was translated to hackamore.

The hackamore principle is similar to that of the snaffle; however, instead of cultivating a horse's mouth, the communication is simply transferred to the horse's nose.

Hackamore men of the old school believed in taking plenty of time and patience in starting a green horse. They contended that it was necessary, once a colt was roughed-out, to keep him "tender." In other words, he was taught to respect the hackamore in the first lesson or two. However, tenderness does not mean soreness. The latter results from rough treatment and bruised tissue. The "tenderness" one wants is the natural sensitivity or responsiveness of a young horse. This can easily be lost by continual yanking and pulling.

"Ride with a loose rein, but maintain contact," was the motto of these trainers. To quote the master, Luis B. Ortega: "A hackamore needs to be firm but flexible to produce good results. It should have life and spring to it, not be just a dead weight. These conditions are determined by the weight and cure of the hide and the type of core the strands are braided over. The body must not be limber or flabby because then the hackamore is practically useless. This limberness may be due to a poor grade of material or poor workmanship. A hackamore braided from strands that are cut from a poorly-cured hide will droop downward, front and back, from the headstall after only a little use."

Ortega goes on to say that, "By poorly cured hide, I mean one that has had the fiber broken down so there is no life or body left. The same results come from a salted hide, or ranch hides that have been thrown over the fence and scorched by the sun. Strands cut from a good hide can be pulled down tightly when braided. This cannot be done with the former type of hide. The stiffness of the hackamore is designed to balance with the nose button and heel knot. The professional hackamore craftsman knows these fine points of construction from years of experience, under all kinds of range conditions, and on many horses."

You seldom find a man that has devoted his lifetime to a trade—in this case, making hackamores—who is willing to reveal his secrets. However, the old *vaquero*, M. R. Valdez, who gave me one of my first lessons, stressed the importance of tight braiding, the tying of the hackamore ends, and of beveling the strands. The reason for the bevel is to eliminate the sharp, raw edge that will work or cut on the horse's chin.

Opinions differ among hackamore men as to results obtained from varying positions of the hackamore on the nose. I believe the beginner and the rider with limited experience will find it better to stick to the generally accepted position: where the raised part of the nose button rests four or five inches above the nostrils and about one to one-and-one half inches above the tender spot where the cartilage joins the bone of the nose. The exact position is based upon the size of the nose button itself and upon the angle of the cheeks.

One needs to keep in mind that horses' heads vary in size. The cartilage joint is your guide; be careful not to injure this spot or kill the sensitivity. Occasionally the wrong position may result in head-tossing, especially if the button rests on a tender spot all the time.

The fault may lie in the hackamore being too heavy and causing too much pressure on the nose. This can be eliminated by raising or lowering the hackamore a little, but the best remedy is to change to a lighter one. Another indication that the hackamore may be too heavy is when a horse will not step out at a good free walk, but instead will hesitate and hold back. A rider should be able to feel this.

To the old-timers, care taken in adjusting the hackamore, and caution exercised in its use, were two important requirements for obtaining the desired training results. Hackamores need to fit the individual horse, and be handled with the same finesse as a snaffle bit.

The Upper and Inner Mouth

Nature gave the horse a mouth with which to assimilate food. Man has taken that mouth and used it as an aid to make the horse do what he wants, whether it be riding, driving, or working him from the ground. The mouth serves the horse one way and man in another. But man, too often, has not taken the time to understand either function of the horse's mouth. He neglects having the teeth floated regularly, having the wolf teeth pulled, or knowing that teeth come out at certain ages. He fails to learn about types of feed the horse can handle with his eating mechanism so that the horse benefits from his food.

The other area of remiss is in the training and understanding of how a horse's mouth functions and what needs to be done to use it properly. My friend and one of the top trainers in the world of "reined horses," Bob Loomis, probably explains the use of the mouth better than anyone I've ever visited with. He puts it in these terms: "The mouth is a telegraph station or a tattletale on all other working parts of the horse's body. It will tell you which parts are working properly and which ones aren't, if you care to pay attention.

"The mouth ties in the drive line from the poll through the neck, shoulders, and rib cage (or body) directly to the hindquarters, which is the horse's driving force. To truly educate the horse and make him a winner, you must develop two mouths (besides the one he eats with). You need an 'upper mouth' where you just take the slack out of the reins and get a light response. Then there is the more important 'inner mouth' when you take a hold, applying more pressure. Without these two mouths being cultivated and educated, you can't possibly have a consistent winner."

According to Bob, the educated mouth lets you know if the

horse is moving stiffly, reluctantly, or is out of position at any time. Being out of position for the job at hand means being out of balance. For instance, when going in a circle, even though there is a slight arc, the body through the rib cage must be kept straight. If a shoulder slips out to the right, the hip goes to the left and the horse escapes his balance.

The first place you feel this is in the mouth. If the horse falls out of position to the right, the right side of the mouth becomes heavy or dull. The same is true for the left side. The mouth tells you that more leg aid is needed to straighten the horse up and get him back in balance.

Too often we find that when the mouth gives this message, people don't listen. They simply jerk on the reins in an attempt to lighten the horse up. That is the biggest mistake that can be made. If you truly feel the mouth, you know what part is not working freely and what leg aid you need to apply. But if you keep jerking the horse off the bridle, you'll ruin that communication system so you'll never know.

Bob feels that there is no place in training the horse where jerking on the mouth accomplishes anything but getting you in trouble. The upper mouth is easily understood and witnessed all the time. It is light and responsive when the slack is taken out of the reins gently, and the horse gives to the hand light and willingly. Because the horse's body works on a swivel, he is fluid, graceful, and well-balanced on a light rein. Many times in showing this is enough, unless the going gets tough and conditions are not just right.

"This happens more often than not," Bob says. "The ground may be too deep or heavy, the arena too small or too large, and distractions from the outside may take the horse's mind off what he's doing. Anything that allows or forces the horse to escape the upper mouth puts you in a position of no mouth, no balance, and no control. The horse may throw his head up, stick his nose out, and escape the bridle (or poll flexion), or over-flex and put his head on his chest. Either way, the communication system has been severed."

Bob believes that if you have cultivated the mouth to the next stage—educated it to go beyond and into the inner mouth—the horse can handle any situation and not escape. He'll give to the pressure and remain balanced, light, and fluid. The fully educated inner mouth takes time, with many hours of riding in the snaffle and using impulsion to drive the horse up into the bridle. The leg works with the hand to create balance.

When this position occurs, you'll find the horse puts his head in a position that provides for optimal performance. To keep him in that position, the rider must determine how much impulsion it takes to ride the horse's head into position. Every horse varies depending on his conformation and attitude.

"Developing the inner mouth is not done by bitting up the horse in a stall," says Bob, "because under those conditions, there is not impulsion; hence, no balance. As the training progresses on good ground, and the horse responds easily to the upper mouth, it is then necessary to increase the pressure in the training process." He suggests a little deeper ground or a little more hold, but always accompanied by an equal increase in impulsion to allow the horse to feel the hand and vice versa. When the horse continues to give, then you are reaching the inner mouth.

"Reach it and back off. Reach it, hold it a little, and back off," Bob advises. "Continue to increase the time you can hold the horse between your hand and your legs. Don't overdo it. Go into it and out . . . easy with the hand, increase the leg, hold with the hand.

Never jerk the horse's mouth for any reason, or you'll never have an inner mouth working for you. This method is like using dressage at an upper level. The horse, on request, becomes responsive, light, and supple at all gaits, and transitions."

Bob's advice is to never let the horse think he can't do something. Cultivate the mind by cultivating the mouth. This will result in a feeling of confidence. A good inner mouth relaxes the mind. The horse understands position because it is taught from the first schooling. If you want a consistent winner, you must cultivate, not force, the mouth.

From Hand to Mouth

We've learned to turn halter horses out fit to a "T"—so well prepared, they could be honored guests at a black-tie affair. Some of us have learned how to slide a horse thirty to forty feet and turn so fast you lose count. We've even mastered the art of jumping a horse over a prescribed course of various fences, demanding perfection at every obstacle.

There is one area, however, that's actually losing ground. The age-old craft of cultivating the horse's mouth, or "putting him in the bridle," seems to have been skipped over in a lot of cases. Too many of us don't seem to care what a horse does or doesn't do with the bit. People talk about the "handle" they have on their horse, but in reality it's a forced, resentful situation they have produced, rather than the kind, giving one I think everyone desires. Horses that "fight their face" just can't get the job done as well as those that give to the bridle.

I don't wish to belabor the "old days" routine, but there was a time when care was taken to have a horse comfortable in the bridle—any horse: pleasure, reining, hunter, jumper, horsemanship, or driving. The horseman always took pride in how his horse responded to his hands.

Hands were talked about; good ones were praised and heavy ones ridiculed. A horseman's hands were among his greatest assets. Maybe along the way we've created scores of technicians and mechanics, but few real horsemen. The business has grown so fast over the past several years that the supply of horses has become greater than horsemen can comfortably handle. This has allowed the quick-fix technician to filter in among the well-educated professionals.

From my vantage point in the arena, I'm surprised at the apparent lack of interest in the mouth. Reiners, as well as a handful of individuals in other divisions, have put a great deal of emphasis on keeping a horse light and responsive to the bridle. But for the most part, there's an absence of concern, or perhaps it's knowledge that's lacking. It seems strange to me that a trail horse that doesn't respond to the bit with sensitivity and dispatch is expected to handle itself as efficiently as one that does. But I see few people in trail classes spending time on the simple basics of cultivating the mouth, or even thinking or talking about it.

Driving horses continually pose a problem because they often don't respond to the driver. It stands to reason the only contact the driver has with the horse is through the lines to its mouth, no matter what kind of harness or buggy, or how inexpensive or costly it may be. Then we have horses going to fences "in combat," trying to get away from the bridle—shaking their heads, rooting their noses —which hinders their ability to jump properly. Horses that you can't take a little hold on are not balanced. Light contact means more than just tension on the reins; it means responsiveness, and lightness of mouth and hands.

In the past, we've seen most of the concentration placed on jerking the mouth—see-saw, jerk, bump, jerk again—as standard procedure for the warm-up, especially in pleasure classes. The quiet mouth will definitely be the next concern in the evolution of the pleasure horse and will most assuredly result in a horse that is able to "wear the bridle" and "handle some." Many pleasure horse aficionados ignore the cultivation of a good mouth; in fact, many have never even felt the mouth. For them, steel of one shape or another simply hangs there to sort of herd the horse around the arena rail. Then in the line-up, they give a quick bump or jerk so the horse will back a few steps when the judge comes by. In the future, we'll be asking pleasure horses to do a little more. This will force communication between the rider and his horse and will let the horseman who understands his horse's ways and needs rise to the top. How well the horse responds to the bridle (à la the reiners) will be the definite edge in days to come.

Trainers used to spend long hours, devote much concentration, and place special emphasis on the horse in the bridle. Unaffected by the pressures of today's show business, owners were a little more patient, and the show didn't go on every day all year long. So it was probably easier to put a good mouth on a horse and keep it that way. Today, we're faced with bringing new ones along quickly. Trainers ride only briefly before letting their assistants take over. Despite this, however, the needs of the horse have remained as they always were. There never has been, and there will never be, a viable shortcut to putting a lasting mouth on a horse.

Those of us inside the ring, whose duty it is to decide which horse and rider teams are best, are talking more and more about what really makes a winner. Our main topics of conversation focus on the question of how the horse moves, handles, and behaves in the bridle. We've bred a tremendous amount of good, athletic horses that are capable of performing, and now it's up to us to find the time and knowledge to teach them properly.

This age of electronic technology allows us to do many things more rapidly, but the need for time in the saddle, patiently feeling the horse's mouth, hasn't changed. Naturally, some horses respond faster than others, just as some classes put more emphasis on the mouth and immediate response than others. Much of the winning advantage, however, will exist in the quiet, responsive, well-trained mouth. When this is realized, and it will be shortly, we can expect a resurgence of gimmicks for people who are continually looking for a speedier way. The solution will be found in educating the assistants who spend their time riding, and in emphasizing the need to develop a horse's mouth. This will necessitate availing ourselves of the so-called "old-timers' " knowledge of just how one puts, and *keeps*, a good mouth on a horse.

The concepts must sift down to our youth, the professional trainers of tomorrow. They need to understand what the bit is for and how to use it. Each bit has a purpose; each horse needs something different; each job requires modifications; and every stage the horse goes through requires change and adjustment. The continuing process of keeping the horse happy in the bridle seeks a profitable goal. When a horse is happy, it will go in balance and have expression . . . two of the traits needed to win any type of competition. *That* knowledge is the key to maintaining a horse in the bridle throughout its show ring career.

Hand Rhythm and Body Weight

With all the conversation going on about "head set," "light in the bridle," and "good mover," I'm often surprised when I witness the misuse of the rider's position on the horse. Many times the rider's position is an out-and-out hindrance. Maybe we haven't put enough emphasis on how the horse reacts to "hands and seat."

Hand rhythm and body weight are extremely important in affecting how a Western horse performs. In a circle, for example, your hands must be in rhythm with the horse's head and you must be in balance with his body. The horse should allow you to stay straight up and down in the saddle, guiding him with just a suggestion of a rein, so he'll remain in balance and position. It's the same thing going down the straightaway—his head is moving, you're going in a straight line, and sitting straight up.

Teaching a horse to lope straight lines and round circles are two of the most important things in training. If a horse wants to fade to the outside of the circle, you should be able to pick up the outside rein and move the shoulder back into the circle. You don't have to be forceful with the rein; just ask him, and squeeze him over with your outside leg. The horse's nose is controlled with your inside rein and his shoulder with the outside rein. You lift up your inside rein to tip his nose in slightly, and you bring the outside rein low against his neck to put the shoulder down. Your outside leg squeezes him to shift his ribcage to the inside.

The use of your weight has a lot to do with guiding a horse. It's like carrying a bucket of water in your right hand—if you have the weight in your right hand, you're going to lean to the left to counterbalance that weight. When you're in the middle of the horse, you are controlling his center of gravity, and if you lean inside, he's going to lean outside to counterbalance you, and vice versa. If he's leaning that way, he's going to turn that way more easily. This is most evident on green horses who just respond to something with no preconceived idea in their mind.

When a horse wants to drift toward the barn or the gate (say you're going around to the left, and he wants to drift to the right), you can shift your weight to the right side, ask him with your hands to go to the left, and he'll go on around to the left. But if you move your weight to the inside (to the left), he'll shoot off to the gate. It's the same thing when you're loping a circle and a horse wants to cut in on you a little bit. By leaning to the inside slightly, getting your weight down on the inside and lifting up with that inside rein, you can keep him from falling in, because he'll lean out and stay out. If he wants to veer out, just shift your weight to the outside a little and drive him to the inside of the circle.

Again, what you're after is to stay straight up and down, and to keep the horse between the bridle reins. That's the ultimate achievement in training. But you can use weight adjustment to help yourself along to that point, and compensate for what the horse is doing more easily. What you want is just a slight shift of weight, so he'll lean the other way just a bit. It's better to have a horse cutting to the inside of his circle rather than fading out all the time. The inside problem is a lot easier to fix than the fading out.

Hand rhythm, balance, and consistency will make your circles comfortable. If you're inconsistent about loping circles, you'll end up with half your circle having a flat side and the other half being cupped. In the reining pattern, for instance, it's so much prettier to see circles that are the same size, with everything symmetrical, and the lead change right across the middle. Teaching a horse its leads involves shoulder control again. When the young horse is walking or jogging in a circle, whichever way he wants to lean with his shoulders is the lead he will take. If you're circling to the right, and his shoulders are stuck out to the left, he'll take that left lead. But if you wait until he shifts his weight to the right, and then ask for a lope, he'll take that right lead.

A rider's hand must be in rhythm with a horse's head. There are different ways to adjust that rhythm to accomplish certain things on a horse, and a lot of what it takes has to be developed by feel over time. When a horse is galloping, for example, and you have to move a shoulder in or out, if you do it in rhythm with the horse, you can do it more easily than if you just take hold of the horse with a dead pull. When he's loping, his head is moving on every stride, and if you have a really fixed hand, the horse is bouncing his mouth on the bit. But if you do it in rhythm, you can pick him up and move him—"ease him over" so to speak—and more is accomplished with less effort.

When a horse lopes, his head bobs up and down in a characteristic, steady rhythm. The rider can watch the top of the head, and as it goes down, he should extend his elbows and hands the same amount down the rein toward the horse's mouth. Another way to gauge this is to look at the saddle horn. The withers and saddle horn have a back-and-forth motion at a gallop. The rider can extend his hands the same distance as, and in motion with, the horn and he'll be synchronized with the horse's mouth. At the trot, there is some bounce, but a horse's head doesn't move much. Even at a walk, though, the horse's head has a motion. However, it flows when he's loping or galloping, and that's the gait in which it's most critical.

Once a horse is trained to give to pressure (break at the poll and drop his nose), when you lift your hand up toward your chest with both reins together, he'll drop his nose back. If you lift your hand straight up with one rein and leave the other slack, he'll tip his nose around to the side. This is especially true when you begin steering a horse with a shanked bit. You don't ever want to pull out wide like you would on a ring snaffle, because you've got that leverage there. If you pull out wide, the bottom of the shanked bit is going to pry the top of the bit into the side of the horse's face and he's going to fight his head. But if you lift your hand up and he feels that little sensation of a backwards pull on the side, he'll tip his nose, turn his head, and go into it from there. That's why the pull should be more up, instead of out, when you're working with a curb.

If you have your hands down low, when you release the pressure, the horse is likely to stick his nose almost straight out, whereas if you want him to drop his nose and put his head down, you lift up more. A horse has a tendency to go in the opposite direction of the pressure you're applying. So the idea of "low hands, low head," with constant jerking, is a fallacy. Make it easy for the horse to move with the rider's weight. Light hands simply means understanding the rhythm of the horse's head movement along with being sympathetic to this natural need.

A Breathtaking Program

Quiz: What is the most overlooked basic when training horses? Give up? Well, the answer happens to be "Air," that single ingredient one cannot survive without.

Much has been said about conditioning the horse, both physically and mentally, but in actual practice few people think about or seem to care about lung capacity, or a horse's ability to breathe. This must be taught and conditioned in order for a horse to increase its ability to function properly. More classes are lost because the horse runs out of "gas" than for any other reason. We demand so much more from our horses today in the show ring and in their preparation that we must not neglect the simple function of breathing. We have all kinds of theories and apparatus to condition the horse—some without concussion, some with calisthenics, many with special diets—but none with simply teaching the proper use of air.

Time after time, and especially in the warm-up area, I see horses being schooled and schooled and they're all gasping for air. Just one more run and stop, just one more spin, one more jump, one more lope around the track—it goes on until the horse is used up inside and his reserve air supply is gone. Then when the horse is taken into the show ring and he doesn't perform, the rider or trainer gets mad. Nothing can be taught and nothing can be retained or even accomplished when you're tired or out of breath. Yet it's at that time we see the whips come out or the spurs dig deeper, never giving a thought to the fact that the horse's air supply has been used up. Conflict and combat become mother nature's automatic defense and a horse is ruined because he has to breathe and the trainer wouldn't allow time for that.

Racehorse trainers and competitive trail ride or endurance trainers come closest to thinking about increased lung capacity. They work on the air supply, but I've only met a couple of show horse trainers that have a program outlined according to breathing ability. It's such a simple thing to add that it amazes me so few do it. Training programs must be thought out and laid out well in advance.

They should contain breathing exercises to give the horse the "bottom" he needs—the staying power and the reserve he requires when called on to beat the others. I've just come from a circuit of top shows, world and national championships, and I've traced the one ingredient all champions had in common: the ability to put on a strong finish. This can only be done with enough air to carry them through the final phase.

When you, yourself, start to run out of breath, automatically you get a type of claustrophobia or panic—the horse experiences the same thing. So why not do for the horse what we do for ourselves? Just stop for a moment, no matter what you're doing, and let him catch his breath before going on. If this basic is taught from the beginning, it makes future training that much easier. Just as you work on the mind to keep it soft and work on the physical muscle tone to keep it in condition, develop a program for teaching the horse to breathe so he will have that ample air reserve to carry him through to the finish.

As you work your horse, pay close attention to his breathing. Take him to a point just when he starts to breathe heavy; let him rest until he regains all his air, then take him to that point again. Repeat that procedure with every training session, increasing the amount of time between rests until your horse is conditioned from the inside out and able to work for quite a while between needed rests. You've actually taught him breathing by rhythm. Never push him beyond his breathing capacity when training. If you condition him properly, he'll be able to breathe with comfort when performing an entire routine, whether around the arena, over fences, or working the cow.

Some horses actually hold their breath at times when jumping, stopping, or when nervous tension arises. You have to be aware of this if the horse you're showing has this tendency, and you'll have to develop an even greater reserve area if this occurs.

With all of our modern methods, especially in the breeding and raising of horses today, I'm not sure we're not doing a disservice of a kind in the breathing area. In many parts of the country we raise foals in small pens or box stalls. We keep them in confinement in our quest for weanling, yearling, and two-year-old halter wins. By the time we're ready to ride them, we've restricted the natural breathing capacity by never allowing it to develop. To survive in nature years ago, the foal would have had to run up and down hills, cover great distances across plains or deserts, swim rivers or lakes, play with other foals, run, jump, buck—all kinds of things we keep them from doing today. In doing this for his survival, the foal kept increasing his breathing capacity and lung control by the mere fact of having to rough it, thus developing his own air surplus naturally over the course of his growing up years.

For various reasons, most horses today don't have the same opportunity to develop the strengths that are badly needed for surviving the demands of man and the show ring. So if the horse has not had the opportunity to develop naturally, a planned program to develop the weak areas is where a true training program should start. Naturally, the earlier a breathing program can be instituted, the better the horse will be. Increased lung capacity and proper breathing can be taught at any age.

Take jogging for instance. When starting out to jog, the first day you can only run half a block or a few yards. You increase that just a little each day and before you know it, you're ready for the Boston Marathon. It all comes from conditioning the breathing and increasing the capacity—learning how to really get the most out of our lungs. The same thing can be done with the horse. If he's too young to ride, pony him from another horse (unless you have acres of open fields for the foals to run in). When he's old enough, drive him, lunge him—do something to get into a program that forces the use of breathing to continually increase his reserve. When the challenge comes it can be met with ease, and more horses will go on to achieve what their other abilities will allow.

We take all the "try" out of a horse when we take away his air. Watch the horses at the next show you attend. Watch how they breathe and when they breathe. Watch the winners who have breath left and watch the losers who leave it all in the warm-up area, or who have never conditioned the breathing at all. Then watch your own horse and see if he has developed the breathing capacity he needs. If he hasn't, start a program today. In fact, we might even hang a title on it and call it "air conditioning."

Judging with 360-Degree Vision

During this past busy year of judging nearly every week, I decided to do a little survey of my own as I went along. I watched the judges who were officiating with me and talked with those whose paths I happened to cross outside the ring. The subject matter or question I posed was, From what position or vantage point is the best place to judge?

As each of their ideas emerged, at the next opportunity I would march right over to that particular spot and analyze the class from that perspective. I've always been an advocate of "what you see is what you get," depending on where you're looking and, naturally, what your mind is concentrating on. To my amazement, not only is what you see what you get, but also important is how much others see or don't see. Some actually handicap themselves by their judging position, to say nothing of handicapping the exhibitor by where they look. My study concluded that all too often, the spectator/exhibitor sees more than the judge. This, as you can see, leads to all types of problems and criticism.

The horse business is based on tradition and steeped in "the way we've always done it." This may or may not be the most beneficial answer to a problem. Sometimes modern technology or a willingness to change makes a lot of sense. Going back to the basics, we as judges are trying to pick a winner who in our opinion is the best horse in the class, and everyone agrees to that. But *how* we view a particular horse in a class definitely will influence our opinion.

Starting with halter classes, historically (as judges), we view the horses coming to us from the in-gate, whether they have all come in and lined up as a group or are coming toward us one at a time. However, the spectators or exhibitors see either the hind view or the side view first, and some from a near front. That really is of no consequence. What *is* important is that the judge views the horse in the best environment and not just by rote.

If you're looking directly into the sun (if judging in an outside arena), you're not going to see the same things you would if the light were coming over your shoulder. If the arena slopes downhill to where you are standing, you're at a disadvantage when allowing horses to stand-up on a slant. The arena must be used to your advantage regarding sun, terrain, silhouette on the wall, or any other situation that could cause a distortion in your viewing.

Inside the arena is still the best and only place to judge halter horses with any degree of accuracy. Performance classes are an entirely different story. After trying every conceivable position except standing on my head, I have made some startling discoveries. Inside the ring, you see a completely different horse show than you do from outside. Another revelation is that at arena floor level you also have a different perspective than when you're a little elevated.

The worst possible place to judge a pleasure or rail class of any kind is inside the ring by the in- or out-gate, facing into the corner. It has always been my contention that an arena encompasses some form of a 360-degree oval, rectangle, or open field, but still the judge has the obligation to see as much as possible of the entire class. The major problem areas for rail horses happen by the gate and in the corner. If a judge simply looks at that one spot, he or she is obviously trying to catch mistakes or more than likely force them. He sees one or two horses at a time and for only a couple of strides—the epitome of tunnel vision. Instead of seeing 360 degrees, it's more like only 10, with the rider being able to stop and have lunch in the remainder of the 350 degrees before making a pass.

The next worst place to view a rail class is to stand, facing the rail, whereby you only see a profile for a few strides. Fifteen or twenty degrees is still not seeing the entire class, and definitely not seeing what others are capable of observing. This is not a new concept, as we've been encouraging judges (at every judge's seminar) to stand in a corner just off the rail facing the majority of the ring in order to view horses coming toward them, going away, and from a profile angle. This view encompasses a greater portion of the class, using 350 degrees and causing the judge to lose the horses only in the remaining 10 degrees—a short period of time. This same premise holds true for nearly every other individually worked class.

After much thought and a lot of trial and error, my conclusion is that nearly all classes (except halter, trail, and cutting) are better judged from outside the ring, almost to a corner and slightly elevated to at least the height of the average horse's eye. Hunter and jumper classes should be judged from a slightly higher position and in the middle of one side of the arena. This allows a broadside view or profile of the horse going over the fences. This, coupled with the position on the opposite side of the arena from the in-and-out or combination, allows the best possible judging view.

Judging the reining classes from much the same position as the hunter gives a better view of how a horse uses the arena, the size and symmetry of the circles, the smoothness and length of the run-down, a much better view of the turn-around, and an easier place to count the number of spins. Also, the judge's view is exactly the same as the spectator/exhibitor . . . in truth, you can just plain old see more.

The advantage in the rail classes, whether judging the horse or the rider, is that no one needs to wander around to see the whole ring. There is no ten degrees out of sight; all horses get looked at equally (unless a judge wants to just focus on one as he goes around). Another obvious advantage for viewing the class just outside and elevated is the ability to see across the arena when there is a gazebo or judge's stand in the center. The distraction of people moving about and activity going on in the center while the horses are performing is lessened.

There are still some disadvantages at this time, until the physical needs are determined; primarily the fact that at most shows today, the only place outside and elevated is in the stands, with others moving or milling about, talking, peeking over your shoulder, etc. These issues are easily handled by having a ringmaster with the judge and an area of seats set aside. At those shows where seats in the stand are nonexistent, I've found that the bed of a pickup truck with a couple of chairs (à la most cutting competitions) parked just outside the ring is a workable solution.

In fact, at some shows in Europe, the judge sits in a judge's car or truck bed with a glass enclosure, table, chairs—the works—and a driver to position the official wherever the best view is deemed to be. I hope this will become a trend of the future here. What you see is definitely what you get, wherever you are.

The Mad Hatters

"It's not what you wear but the way that you wear it"—a well-meaning cliché and especially true where hats are concerned. In fact, there are songs about hats, stories about hats, jokes about hats, and even a cowboy superstition that is religiously followed: Never put your hat on the bed.

Observation can provide insight to a person's character by the hat they wear: type, size, color, and most of all *shape*, can tell a lot about personality, particularly in the horse business.

From my vantage point in the arena, I see everything imaginable, from top hats to derbies, snap brims to cowboy hats. Each, by its individuality, sets the stage. The borrowed hats, too big, encircling the ears and sometimes eyes, never moving even when the rider's head turns. The scarred hunt cap with velvet trim, worn by some as a badge of courage, but to the judge an indication the rider has fallen off a lot.

In no division is the hat so distinctive or characteristic of the person as in the Western classes. Each discipline has its own basic style—the cutting horse crease, the reiner style. Even the breeds have hats peculiar to that breed. When you meet someone with a cowboy hat, you can tell whether they're "urban" or "for real," simply by the make and shape, and most assuredly, by the care a true horseman gives to his hat.

If you want to "pull back a bloody stump," just take hold of a horseman's hat the wrong way. There's an unwritten law about cowboys' hats. They're revered, even cherished, and always protected.

One of the known hazards when wearing a cowboy hat is traveling on an airplane. Unfortunately, most passengers do not share the owner's tender regard for his hat. If you place it in the overhead rack, you face the possibility of having it crushed beyond recognition by those careless beings who throw jackets, luggage, and other articles into the compartment without looking to see what has been placed there beforehand. I just keep my hat in my hand until everyone is seated, then I place it gingerly someplace where it will be cradled like a newborn baby.

A hat may become a little soiled but should never be out of shape. Hours are spent by the wearer, shaping or reshaping to maintain its character.

Many horsemen actually use their hats as trademarks, not only for their distinctive shapes, but also for their color. Not the gaudy colors like blue, green, yellow, or red, but the basics: black, silver-belly, buckskin, sterling, mink, and the like. The true hat wearer knows what brand fits him the best, what crown height and brim width goes with his image.

Rodeo contestants' hats also have their own look, quite different from the pleasure horse enthusiasts.

Most horsemen, by nature, have superstitions. Favorite hats for certain classes, dressy hats for going out, and comfortable hats to work in. Some people, though, have little regard for their hat, which really grates on most of the judges I've visited. The gymkhana rider is one. Even though the rules allow for this, he rides into the arena and immediately throws his hat off. This happens to irritate a ringmaster friend of mine so badly that he will walk over, pick up the hat, and toss it over the fence into the cow pen. Yup, his one burning desire is to have it walked on and manured under. If the contestant has no more regard for his hat than to toss it off, then neither does he.

The cowboy hat is worn with pride by those in the business and becomes an invitation to converse with those you meet along the way whose hats divulge the same interests. It's sort of a calling card. More often than not, the one who looks the part can play the part, and nearly always those who don't have a clue as to how the hat should be worn give the same impression when performing. Regardless of the horse, it's pretty hard for the (horseman) judge to place a rider that has his hat on backward or wears a hat with the back of the brim curled up as if it had been put on a shelf and crushed from behind.

The shape of hats or the way they're creased has changed over the years, according to fad, but the basics and the way they're worn have not. You can walk into a room and look at the hats hanging on the wall and immediately tell what kind of a group you're in. Horsemen, of what kind—gunsels or pseudos, trail riders or showmen—it's all there on the hat rack.

The cowboy hat has become acceptable in all horse show disciplines—you see as many in the hunter-jumper ranks behind the scene as you do at the Western shows. Judges of all breeds have taken to the cowboy hat, each with its own particular breed style. Hats can be so distinctive that people are actually remembered by their hat rather than their name.

I had an experience that's still talked about by the organizers of the National Horse Show held at Madison Square Garden. Now, for a Burbank-raised horse trainer to be invited to judge The Garden was like a dream come true. This was several years ago but it's still referred to as if it just happened. When you judge The Garden, you must wear white tie and tails and a top hat for all evening performances, and a morning suit (gray tails and gray top hat) for daytime classes. I had no trouble renting the tails and a black topper, but for the life of me, I couldn't locate a gray top hat for my daytime duties.

As usual, I had waited until the last moment, frantically calling every tux rental shop in southern California, but to no avail. Then, as usual, I had a brainstorm—Hollywood! They must, I reasoned, use gray top hats in the movies. So, thumbing through the Yellow Pages, I decided "Western Costume" was the solution. I dialed. Sure enough, one gray top hat was available and rentable. It didn't matter that it was one size larger than I normally wear. I could stuff paper in the brim—as long as it was gray.

I picked it up the morning we left; it was sealed in a crushproof box, ready for jetting to New York. I thought no more of the hat until I was dressing for the show the next morning. Untying the string, I opened the top of the box. I didn't know whether to laugh or cry, for there in the box was *the* very hat that could have been worn by W.C. Fields, or maybe the Mad Hatter, or both! I had no choice; off to the show it went. My hat in hand, I entered the arena with the other judges and stood for the introductions. As we lined up together, the ringmaster placed us in groups according to the classes we were to judge. I stood with Kenny Wheeler who measures about 6'2". He was introduced and put his hat on. I was next, blossoming to my full 5'9". The ringmaster came over and said, "Don, put your hat on." I complied.

Murmuring undertones crept through the audience, quickly replaced by polite chuckles and a few outright guffaws. With my top hat perched on my head, I had miraculously become as tall as Kenny—the two top hats were level!

I've been invited to judge The Garden again this year, but with one request—not to bring the same top hat. They said they'd be happy to rent one for me.

Riding Lessons

A while back I became acquainted with a psychologist of some fame. He told me his eleven-year-old daughter had received a series of riding lessons as a birthday gift. I ran into him again about a year later—the story about his first year in the horse business just has to be told.

His life had been quite normal prior to this: an office in a prestigious location, golf every Saturday with a guaranteed starting time, and an occasional round on Wednesday afternoon. Sunday was generally a quiet day doing something with family and friends.

After the birthday party, the riding lessons were routinely scheduled on Saturday mornings. Mom would take her so nothing would interfere with Dad's golf date. In fact, he thought it was ideal, because it gave his wife something to do (as if she needed something else to do) while he played. After a round or two, he would come home and be filled in on the exciting tales of one learning to ride. After the third lesson, the conversation not only occupied Saturday afternoon, but all day Sunday, too. "Horse talk all the time," he said, "and it became a normal topic for dinner as well."

The following Saturday, a sore back canceled the golf game. This misfortune just happened to fall on the day of the final gift riding lesson. Because of all the enthusiasm that only an eleven-year-old can muster, he decided to witness the miracle of a natural rider emerging from one who stumbled over furniture and hung all her clothes on the floor.

Naturally, both mother and daughter had been coaxing him to extend the lessons for a few more weeks, just to satisfy a hunger that was growing in a youngster eager to succeed. As a psychologist, he should have sensed what was coming, but, as he said, he was oblivious to any outside force changing his lifestyle.

Arriving at the stable, he was met by the instructor, who proceeded to tell him how much potential his daughter had. "A natural born rider with the ability to be a champion," was the way he put it. I could picture it all: the teacher talking; the father's chest swelling while telling others watching the lesson, "That's my daughter over there (gesturing), only four lessons! She's a natural athlete, you know . . . takes after me."

No further encouragement was needed. Immediately after the lesson, pen in hand, Dad was signing up for the next series. Not with a group, though, because his daughter was so talented, she should have private lessons. The "privates" were given on Friday and Sunday, so why not one of each? After all, he could well afford it, and it seemed to make everyone in the family happy.

Things progressed; the enthusiasm and horse talk now began to drift into conversations at the office. Seems some clients had children who rode, and some even won ribbons at an event called a horse show. It just so happened his daughter's lesson was canceled on Sunday because they were having one of these horse shows. So, to keep her from missing out, the teacher came up with a solution: Why not let her rent the horse she was riding for the day? She could enter a couple of classes, just for experience. The die was cast!

Sunday came and everyone was ready for the debut, even Grandma and Grandpa. They arrived to find other riders in special clothes, not the old jeans and worn-out boots their daughter wore for lessons. The teacher, quickly searching for a remedy, hustled around and found some clothes that would do.

My psychologist friend didn't know equitation from pleasure, but when the dust settled, his little rider had ended the day with a ribbon. Yellow was the most exciting color ever invented, and again, if he had noticed, a sign of a changing lifestyle.

"Third place," he kept saying, "and after only a couple of months!" Not only did every member of the family in six states hear about it; so did everyone in his golf club and his office building, including patients. His instructions to his family (Mom, that is) as he left for the office Monday morning, ribbon in briefcase, were: "Go wherever you have to go and get her the proper outfit, the best they have. There may be another show coming up."

And, another show coming up, there was. This time it was a few miles away and was to be held on both Saturday and Sunday. Because he was a dutiful husband and father (and also hooked), he got a substitute for his Saturday foursome, made arrangements to lease the horse for two days, plus hauling, and had his secretary reserve a motel room.

Show day arrived and they were overwhelmed—it seemed so much bigger than the local stable show. There were more horses and riders, even some pros. But there they were, in the new clothes right out of the store window. They laugh today at what they must have looked like to the old-timers.

Saturday pulled a blank: The star of the family got on the wrong lead, went off-course, couldn't walk, and almost got run off with. That night my friend was properly filled in on why his precious hadn't done so well by a trainer who had all the answers.

"Now, for starters," began the trainer, "the way you're dressed . . . everyone knows you haven't been around much, and lesson horses are fine for lessons. But for shows, well, that's another matter. In fact, at this show where points are concerned, you have the best riders in town competing."

84

"Points? What are points?" was the father's main question at the time. After several hours of orientation with the trainer, he understood what horse showing was all about. First, buy a horse, put it in training, and take lessons every day. The trainer, always willing to help, just happened to have a horse for sale that, well, might be brought over to try on Sunday in the special class of the day. The class was for novice riders who'd never won a ribbon of any kind at a recognized show.

"But she got third a couple of weeks ago," was the honest revelation by the father. "That was a schooling show," the trainer countered, "not recognized by anyone, so she's still eligible."

On Sunday the horse came, as promised (for an additional fee). "Tense" described everyone as the class got underway. Trainer and instructor gave advice as the rider went from gait to gait. "The judge seems to like her," the trainer told the father, adding, "The horse really fits; it's a good combination."

As the ribbons were awarded there arose a spontaneous cheer. "All right!" burst from the doctor's mouth as a red ribbon was awarded to his pride and joy! Driving home, the ribbon hung from the rearview mirror as the family talked incessantly about the horse they had just bought.

As he continued to tell me of his first year in the horse business, I visualized . . . gone are the golf clubs and the quiet Sundays. They'd been traded for weekends at horse shows, along with two new horses (you can't expect one to do it all), new wardrobes for every division, and a motorhome in which to change clothes. All of a sudden it seemed to come to him, he said. There he was at a horse show—cold, wet, dirty, standing in line waiting to get a hot dog (you had to slop on your own mustard and relish), staring at a trash can lined with flies, asking the lawyer-father in front of him if someone should get a can of fly spray, and reflecting on the cost of those ribbons. Not miserable, but loving every moment; enthusiastic and jubilant at what was being accomplished.

He began to wonder why. So he went to see a psychiatrist friend of his and spent several sessions relating how his life had been changed by a simple birthday gift. The psychiatrist actually concluded, in jest, that he was crazy. But, because of it all—good and bad, winning and losing, pulling together for a common goal—he and his family were closer and happier than they'd ever been.

And, so the story goes: The psychiatrist, having had second thoughts, decided that maybe riding lessons would be a good gift for his daughter, too. So, having taken the bait, they are now clearly heading down the same path of no return to their first horse show!

At Last! Spectators

A t last, a welcome phenomenon has hit the horse show
world—lots of spectators! Reining and the road to Glad-
stone has certainly proven this to be true. At the USET Festival,
the spanking new reining arena presented by the American Quarter Horse Association was dedicated, and reinings took place, from
Free Style and Pro Am to the Cosequin $100,000 championship
presented by Bayer.

It is being discussed in some of the strangest places; cocktail
parties, sit-down dinners, advertising agencies, and even among talent scouts. People are becoming aware that the word "show" shares
the spotlight with "horse" when the contest becomes a horse show.
Some managers or equine entrepreneurs are truly making their
productions fall into the show category.

For years we've heard the naysayers claim, "Horse shows are just
not spectator sports. Who wants to sit and watch a bunch of
horses slowpoking around the arena hour after hour?"

In Europe, show jumping has been one of the best attended
spectator sports. Their television coverage carries every round and
detail much like football or baseball here. Kids even line up after
the show to collect an autograph of their favorite rider. Even
though it's a game and not a horse show contest, polo in South
America attracts large audiences just as rodeo for years has taken
the lead in horse-related sports in the United States. The craze is
just now reaching the point where this country is beginning to
televise horse showing.

Not every horse contest can be an extravaganza. We need a
place to show all of our horses in every type of competition; the
playdays or schooling shows, the circuits (a category that most

shows fall into), the fairs and expositions. But we need the spectators, too. To attract them, we need more than a place where horses and riders are invited because of their standing in the ranks. A few classes that are exciting to watch, sprinkled in among other acts or events thrilling in their own right, helps to draw a crowd.

Over time, exhibitors have become a bit myopic by only showing to each other day after day. This habit has brainwashed many into thinking that's what horse shows are all about. Maybe we should look into what can be done, even at home, to encourage spectators to attend.

One simple example is to stop keeping everything a secret. We know what's happening but no one else does. How can we expect a newcomer to the horse world to understand the logistics of every class when (at some shows) the announcer is only allowed to read a number. If we tell about a horse or rider and their accomplishments during the performance, some conclude we may be influencing the judge. So we say nothing, and the new spectator watches for a moment and then leaves to find a more exciting form of entertainment.

What would be wrong with identifying the up-and-coming new horse challenging the world champion? If managers (as many are doing now) allow a little levity to creep into this serious business, they would be surprised at how the morale at the barn changes.

From my own experience years ago, I had the honor, along with Billy Harris, to judge the "Wayne Newton Classic" held in Las Vegas at the convention center. The crowds were great, especially in a town where gambling, fine food, and the best in entertainment abounds. It was rewarding to see that a horse show in direct competition with all of these diversions could attract 15,000 people for a given performance.

Of course it was invitational with much prize money offered; a horse show event and rodeo event coupled with some top clown acts. When Wayne called us over and asked us to come up with an opening act to warm up the audience, it didn't take long for Billy and I to conjure up something big and unexpected for each night.

The first night the horn blower loaned Billy his coat and me his top hat. We each had a horn and when the spotlight came on in the darkened arena for the class call, we raised our horns high and pretended to play. People started to clap. Billy put his horn down and bowed and I continued giving the impression that I was playing. When I stopped to bow, it was obvious that two clowns (judges) were hamming it up, because the real horn blower (outside the arena) was still sounding the actual "Boots and Saddles."

The next night Billy and I prevailed upon one of the clown acts, whose performance consisted of one clown riding Roman-style into the arena and a second clown appearing and vaulting up to join him. We decided to make a few alterations to the opening and the clowns were eager to comply. When the gate opened, in came two judges and a clown cavorting around the arena, Roman riding on two draft horses.

The final night we were to ride in Benny Benion's stagecoach. Now, having spent some time in business in Vegas, I knew quite a few people and one of them happened to be the animal trainer at Circus Circus. The lights were dim, the spotlight on the coach. It circled and stopped, center stage. As we planned it, the announcer could not see from his vantage point who exited from the stagecoach. He called each by name. "The Honorable Billy Harris." The crowd roared with laughter, as the coach door opened. He continued, "The Honorable Don Burt." More laughter and then applause. The coach door closed and the stage pulled out, leaving the spotlight on two tuxedo-clad chimpanzees holding clipboards, ready to judge. No one was in on the switch, not even Wayne. We had truly stopped the show!

Making History in the Western Horse World

If it had been a gymnastic competition, the score would have been nines and tens. Had it been baseball, a grand slam home run would have been garnered. And if a horse race was the bill of fare, a wire-to-wire win would have been celebrated. That is how the reining demonstration at the World Equestrian Games in Rome was viewed.

Sanctioning a Western horse to participate for the first time was history in the making. Many applications to put on demonstrations were submitted, but only reining was given the green light. It was through the efforts and cooperation of many people, but our elected director from Italy, Antonio Giraudini, and our appointed director, Antonio Mastrangelo, coupled with the AQHA staff and the NRHA, carried the ball.

The demonstration was held in the Stadio Flaminio in downtown Rome just prior to the freestyle dressage event. The day before our debut, the rains came and came, but on Sunday afternoon, October 4th, the sun smiled down on a group of cowboys ready to join the ranks. Unlike dressage competitions, which yield not a whisper from the audience, the reiners' slides and spins produced a crowd that went ballistic. I actually got a frog in my throat watching a dream come true.

There were nine countries represented in the demonstration: Australias Martin Larcombe riding Katie Be Sweet; Canadian Pierre Ouellet on Explosive Missile (Pierre set up the initial meeting); England's Francesca Sternberg on Lightnin Quik Chic; France's Franck Perroet atop Label Me Flashy; Germany's Volker Schmitt riding No Resistance; Holland's Rieky Von Osch on

Commander Flit Fritz; Israeli Elan Rosenberg riding Zan Parr Catalyst; Italian Francesco Arrighi on Arc Sparkle Surprise; and USA's David Hanson on Arc Antares Surprise.

Each country demonstrated a different reining pattern that was accompanied by the commentary of NRHA President Frank Costantini, and AQHA President, Mike Perkins, along with demonstration announcer Simona Diale. The finale, a *pas de deux*, was performed by Marcus Schopfer on Bars Jackson Bo and Dario Carmignani on Olie Dun It Too. The two riders, selected by the Italian Reining Association, performed a mirrored image of pattern #5 to a fitting song, "Run for the Roses." The perfectly synchronized exhibition promptly spurred bravos from a standing audience, and it echoed again as the eleven riders exited the arena.

It was especially gratifying to watch the riders from other disciplines gather on the rail, cheering the maneuvers and admiring what a reined horse can do. That evening, following our crowd-pleasing success, we attended a reception for about 150 dignitaries at the ambassador's mansion. The hospitality of ambassador Thomas Foglietta, along with his impromptu speech praising Western horses (which he rides) and his wishes for the future, was truly a highlight of the trip.

Besides reining, the trip had a few other memorable moments worth noting. During a tour of the Vatican and just outside of the Sistine Chapel, where no talking or pictures are allowed, our tour guide's cell phone began to ring. Naturally all heads in the entire area snapped in her direction. She quickly placed it to her ear and whispered, "Yes." Turning to our group she queried (in broken English), "Is there a Mr. Treadvay in attendance?" We were certain it was the Pope because we had prayed for good weather. But indeed, Antonio Giraudini had tracked us down. I'm sure no other association's Senior Marketing Director has received a phone call at such a holy address.

On several occasions during our trip, we found someone who had seen the demonstration. Glowing compliments never ended. It was covered on television, written about in newspapers and magazines, and talked about in every barn and at every party for the remainder of the Games. While visiting with the riders, I found that they were more nervous putting on the demo than showing in a big futurity; I also believe they became overnight stars to a new audience. Even after returning to the States, the accolades are still coming in from those who were there, including the other disciplines.

The trip back home also had its lighter moments. One incident occurred on our British Airways flight from Rome to England. The two flight attendants who served us had the usual stiff upper lips with dry senses of humor to match. As we were making our descent into Manchester, my wife Ardys was applying some hand lotion. Being told to prepare for landing, she discovered the cap was missing from her tube of lotion. Frantically, she looked all over and her search took her not only out of the seat but under it as well. The flight attendant, sensing something amiss, came to our row and, seeing my wife under the seat, said with a starched upper, "Does she have her seat belt on?" We laughed all the way to the passport window where the agent asked us if we were married. Not having been asked that before, I said, "Why?" He said our frivolity was so abundant, he assumed we were merely traveling companions, in which case my wife would have to step into the other line. We assured him we were *very* married.

Since becoming the sixth discipline of the USET, we are steamrolling ahead. I predict that Western hats and boots, and sliding and spinning, will capture new fans around the world and make reining a new household word.

PART II

REAL
HOLLYWOOD
TALES

Surprise:
First Screen Star Was a Horse!

"How The West Was Won" was an invitation I couldn't refuse. The New York State Historical Association asked me to talk about the "Western Horse," a subject right up my alley. It was to be a full evening—a pre-lecture dinner with the attendees, slides, video, transparencies—the works.

In preparation, I discovered how little I knew about the extent of influence the Western horse has had on all generations of people throughout the history of America. While tracing the cowboy, I found that what was to be known as the West had its beginning in the sixteenth century when the Spanish brought livestock to Florida. Later, around 1611, the British imported cattle to the northern colonies where they developed their own version of cattle culture. The "cattle hunters," as they were called, worked mostly on foot with the aid of dogs and whips.

Herds of one to three hundred head of cattle appeared in the Ohio Valley by the 1800s, and herding techniques had dispersed throughout the South into east Texas. Moving further into west Texas, the Anglo cowboys changed substantially under the influence of the Mexican *vaqueros*. Hence, the real start of the Western horse. At that time it was recalled in a journal that the wild horses had a very unpleasant gait, were capricious, difficult to govern, and even frequently threw their rider and took flight. I've seen a few like that and not too long ago.

The saga of the West spawned trail drives, the railroad, and Wild West shows. I touched on "ridin' for the big money" that grew out of early ranch competitions, the era of the Turtles, and the current world championships and revival of the ranch rodeo as we know it today.

No history of the Western horse would be complete without the movie horse. In fact, the first screen star was a horse in action. Leland Stanford, president of the Central Pacific Railroad, wanted to prove that a trotting horse had all four feet off the ground simultaneously. He employed engineers and scientists to develop a method to show horses in motion. By using a series of cameras placed at short intervals, they were able to prove with moving pictures that trotting and galloping horses did at times have all four feet off the ground.

It was Thomas Edison, though, who really pioneered the movie industry. In 1894, he made a 643-frame celluloid called "Bucking Bronco," featuring Lee Martin of Colorado riding a horse named Sunfish. Subsequently, he produced a 43-foot film entitled "The Burning Stable," a 45-foot sequel, "Fighting The Fire," and a film called "Cripple Creek Bar-Room," depicting Western life. However, the first important drama ever filmed was *The Great Train Robbery*. It was a true Western, even though it was shot entirely in New Jersey.

My audience easily grasped why horses have been so popular and important to the movies. Ever since man first domesticated them, about 3000 B.C., a strong bond has linked man to the horse. I continued to trace the Western horse's popularity through horse shows, trail rides, and basic recreation, and then asked for questions. It was no surprise that horses relating to movie stars were their main focus.

I reminded them that for most of the "B" Westerns, directors preferred solid-colored horses. Bays, blacks, and chestnuts were the most popular. Producers frowned on horses with distinctive markings, such as odd-shaped blazes or irregular spots, because they feared the horse would upstage the actor. Unusual markings also made it difficult to use a double. Because many horses were versatile, a solid color allowed them to be used to play several different parts in the same movie. For example, in one scene, a horse might be used to pull a buggy, but in subsequent scenes would pull a plow, herd cattle, or pull a stagecoach, and no one in the audience would be the wiser.

The white horse has long been emblematic of victory and associated with power, pride, and glory. It became logical then that the good guy (the hero) rode a white horse and wore a white hat. In contrast, the bad guy almost never rode a light-colored horse. Actually, most of the white horses were really gray but their color had lightened with age.

A very famous Western movie scene is of Lee Marvin on a gray horse in *Cat Ballou*. Marvin, as "Kid Shelleen," looks really hung over while sitting on a cross-legged horse and leaning against a building. When accepting an Oscar for his role in *Cat Ballou*, Marvin said, "Half of this belongs to a horse out there in the Valley called Smokey." However, Smokey did receive an award of his own —The Craven Award—for his role in the movie.

The final question needed no research. Without a doubt, the biggest moneymaker was a horse in Fat Jones's string during the forties and fifties. He was a favorite of the stars, but the studios would have to rent all the horses for their movies from Fat Jones in order to get Steel for the star. He was a big chestnut horse with a white-blazed face and three white stockings. You may remember a few of Steel's movies and mounts: Joel McCrea in *Buffalo Bill*, *The Virginian*, and *Four Faces West*; Clark Gable in *The Tall Men* and *Across The Wide Missouri*; Gregory Peck in *Yellow Sky*; Ben Johnson

in *She Wore A Yellow Ribbon, Fort Apache,* and *The Wagonmaster.*
Steel was with John Wayne in *The Conqueror;* Gary Cooper in *It's A Big Country,* and my close friend Robert Taylor in *Westward The Women.* He not only was a truly great horse, but he just happened to be an American Quarter Horse, foaled on Hyde Merritt's ranch in Arizona.

Old Times and Friends

Scrapbooks, feed and tack stores, as well as local cafes and pubs, are all places to reminisce, gossip, or exchange viewpoints. I spent a great deal of my younger years in a place abundant with all of the above. In fact, when you bought a house in one area, called Riverside Ranchos, they gave you a horse to go along with the deal.

Today, the River Bottom of Burbank is still a place beckoning my return . . . roots, I guess. I remember riding across the swinging bridge into Griffith Park when I was five. The bridge still spans the river and is used daily. Most all of the rent stables are gone, the tack shops have changed hands, and the Hitching Post Bar and Jerry Ambler's Amble Inn have been replaced by condos. But horses still manage to be squeezed into every nook and cranny. The Pickwick Coffee Shop remains open, sharing the echoes of trainers, shoers, movie extras, and rodeo greats. Many a cowboy whiled away his time in the River Bottom between rodeos and stunt work.

I took a ride there the other day with some folks who were new to the area and had a great time reliving the history of the horse business. Fickett's Corner housed one arena and an hour down the trail was the Horse Palace, where many people shipped their horses by rail car instead of van. I remembered riding over the Hollywood Hills and down Sunset Boulevard (which then had a bridle path down its center) to show at the Riviera Polo and Country Club or up the hill at Will Rogers Ranch. A horse show was somewhere within riding distance nearly every week.

We rode to a point overlooking what is now Forest Lawn Cemetery, but in the 50s it was Hudkin's Ranch, a movie livestock rental establishment. In the Valley, which made up the largest part of the Ranch, Sunday afternoons were reserved for match races.

Lookouts were posted on the ridge to be on guard for "the cops," as betting was popular sport on 200-yard dashes. Those were the days when you just rode in and struck up a race.

I rode a gray horse then called Dog, owned by Homer Dixon. Dog was the favorite bulldoggin' horse at many rodeos and in that area was about as famous as "Babe," a few years later. My granddaddy had a habit of taking us out of town to show; I always knew when we were going because he would show up at the barn with bib overalls and Brogan shoes, looking like he'd just finished plowin'. We had an old pickup with baling wire hung on the sides of the stock rack. After loading up, we usually headed north, maybe about a hundred miles, where few, if anybody, knew him. We'd find a little show he'd heard about from gossiping at one of his hangouts and he'd enter in some games—barrels, poles, musical chairs, and the like.

He rode an old center-fire stock saddle with a high cantle and would kinda bounce around and interfere with his horse. Being friendly, he'd start conversing with the other contestants, who probably didn't take him too seriously, but before the day was over he would find someone who would match race us. I never did know for how much, but often it was quite a lot for those days.

I'd be kept kinda under wraps until needed, mostly to run for the 200-yards. Somehow Granddaddy would palaver them into thinking he was going to ride and then when it was time, out I'd come weighing probably 95 pounds soaking wet and carrying my race saddle. Naturally my appearance caused a lot of commotion and rhubarbs, but Granddaddy seemed to always win the argument, and after a lap-and-tap start with me in the saddle, Dog and I usually came through. While Granddaddy collected the money, I tended the horse and, if it had been a good day, he'd sing all the way home.

After riding for a couple of hours, we came back to the "Cricket Field," which is now the Grand Prix course at the Los Angeles Equestrian Center. However, back in my era they played cricket on the field while trainers schooled on the perimeter.

We ended up at the local watering hole where more tales flourished as old-timers and locals filtered in. Seems everybody famous in the horse business at one time or another called the River Bottom home, even for a day or two. People could always find a bed and a stall when passing through.

In fact, one of my favorite moments happened right there, during the time when I was helping develop the Equestrian Center. I was busy at my desk one day, waiting for my wife to join me for lunch, when in popped a trio of buddies from way back—Jock O'Mahoney, Ben Johnson, and Yakima Canutt. Now I saw Jocko all the time, and Ben, maybe every couple of years, but I hadn't seen Yak since I was fifteen or sixteen years old. Yakima was close to ninety and still telling spine-tingling tales of the legendary stunts he performed in the movies.

My wife arrived and we all walked to the restaurant where we were greeted by a sign: Please Wait To Be Seated. Yak, either choosing to ignore the sign or not seeing it, proceeded right to the center of the room and sat at the large round table. As the hostess hurried over to intercept us, she recognized my celebrity friends and instead, welcomed us with menus. We ordered a salad here, a sandwich there, and when the waitress came to Yak, he said (with a straight face), "Bring me a side of buffalo and a barrel of whiskey." Stunned for a minute, the waitress looked at Yak, wrote it down, and left. Returning a few minutes later, she announced, "Sorry sir, we're all out of buffalo." Yak slapped his side, settled down to the "diet plate," and our reminiscing began.

Yakima Canutt:
A Cowboy at Heart

To continue down the reminiscing trail with my trio of buddies, Jock O'Mahoney, Ben Johnson, and Yakima Canutt . . . I
decided to do a story on Yak, as he was getting up in years. His
house was nearby in North Hollywood. Like Yak, it was not pre-
tentious, but warm, friendly, and beckoning. Nostalgia floated
around the den touching upon trophies, saddles, photographs, and
awards, finally resting on the mantle where the Oscar Yak won for
the movie Ben Hur proudly stood in the center, surrounded by
other pictures and memorabilia.

We sunk into big comfortable chairs and I asked him about his
colorful career as a stuntman. He actually blushed a little, but a
twinkle came into his eye and he retorted, "Don, most of it you
probably couldn't print." I reassured him I'd leave out the outlaw
traits and then got serious again.

"Most people don't realize you were born Enos E. Canutt about
sixteen miles out of Colfax, Washington, and that you were the
world champion cowboy in 1917, 1919, and 1922. The saddles
you've won have been so numerous you've lost count, except for the
three won at the Pendleton Roundup that hold special memories.

"You were a bronc-ridin' fool, sneakin' out when you weren't
even sixteen so your folks wouldn't find out. Then, at the first
Pendleton you competed in, you earned the nickname you'd carry
for life. Palling around with a couple of cowboys from Yakima
country, you decided to try some broncs out a few days ahead of
the Roundup. Your friends were firm believers in a bit of firewater
to settle their nerves, so you joined them on this occasion. Your
pals were quickly spun off their broncs like toppled windmills, and

took quite a razzing. This spurred you into showing them what a Yakima bronc rider could really do. You climbed aboard, calling loudly, 'Turn this field mouse loose!' They let him go, and that scrawny fuzztail made you look like a rank amateur.

"A photographer had captured you upside down above that bronc and to carry on the ribbing, captioned it 'Yakima Canutt leaving the deck of a Pendleton bronc.' The cowboys picked it up and started calling you 'Yakima,' which was soon cut to 'Yak.' The publicity surrounding this disastrous ride had taught you a good lesson: alcohol and bronc riding didn't mix.

Abiding by this rule from then on (and breaking a few others along the way), you did pretty well. You saw fourteen years of rodeoing, consistently winning the bronc riding in every major rodeo and all the money at Yankee Stadium in the bulldoggin' (now called steer wrestling). In 1923 you won the All-Around and Roosevelt Trophy in Los Angeles. The next thing you knew, you were in pictures and today a legend."

"Seems like you know more about me than I do, Don." Yak said smilingly. "Only the cowboy part . . . now you've got to fill me in on the actor-stuntman phase." I replied.

Yak obliged. "Having met a few screen personalities at the rodeo, I ended up at Fox Studios doing a series of Western action films, affectionately called 'Blood and Thunder Quickies.' Douglas Fairbanks and Tom Mix, along with agents and directors, were instrumental in molding my career during the early Silent Screen era. So, between rodeoing and making a lot of Quickies you've probably never heard of, I kept afloat.

"But along came Talkies, and I found myself in trouble, as did many big name stars. My voice lacked resonance, due to damaged vocal chords from the flu I had while in the Navy. It also coincided with the Great Depression. Sitting up nights, I analyzed what the picture business needed: excitement and thrills. My cowboy background seemed to be a natural fit. You had to think, plan, and analyze your risk. The work came quickly then because I could usually do the stunts on the first take, which saved the producer time and money.

"A stunt has to be well planned out so the danger is kept at a minimum. As you know, Don, I've never had a horse injured in a stunt in all my life. The staging comes next and then the athletic ability. Whether I did the stunt or set it up for others, the stuntman had to be an athlete. Lastly, there had to be an escape plan in case something went wrong."

"Saved my life a time or two," Jocko chimed in.

Ben interjected, "You and John Wayne created the method everyone uses today to do fights so they look natural and real."

Yak sighed. "Yeah, we tried a lot of stuff and camera angles till we got it down pat."

I interrupted, "Yak, the stunt you're probably most famous for is portrayed in the movie *Stagecoach*, with John Wayne.

"A stunt man's dream," he recalled. "I played an Indian making a transfer from a running horse onto one of the lead team horses of the coach. As I'm trying to stop or wreck the coach, Wayne shoots me and I fall between the two speeding lead horses. I'm hanging onto the lead tongue, dragging on my back, when Wayne fires again. I turn loose, letting six horses pass over me—three on each side and then the coach. I rolled over, fell back, and laid still. The director yelled, 'Cut!' I finally hopped up grinning and said, 'I'll be happy to do it again, Mr. Ford, you know I love to make money.' He was sweating and said, 'I'll never shoot that again—they better have it in the can!'

"Looking back over three careers—as rodeo contestant, stunt-man-actor, and action director of motion pictures—I am proud of the accomplishments that placed me in the National Cowboy Hall of Fame and won me the Oscar (which also cited my safety record). But Don, throughout it all, I was just a cowboy at heart, trying to make a living."

Movie Horses

After I published a column about Steel, the horse of choice by many movie stars, I received numerous inquiries about other Quarter Horses used in the picture business. In fact, there was a saying in the heyday of the Western movie: "When the Star needed a star, he chose a Quarter Horse!"

Competition among the Western stars was far-reaching, and each contested to procure a distinctive, easy-to-recognize mount that movie patrons would remember. To share billing, the chosen horse needed certain star qualities: photogenic, pleasing to the eye, graceful, and above all, controllable. Many of the stars turned to the Quarter Horse—an animal that reflected the very traits the hero wished to project.

One of the first movie Quarter Horses to achieve fame was Tony, Jr., the much-publicized horse of Tom Mix. After Mix rode his wonder horse Tony (breeding not known) to earlier fame, he retired him and purchased Tony, Jr. from a New York florist. Tony, Jr. then stepped into the role of super-horse and carried Tom Mix until the end of his career. When Mix was killed in an automobile accident, Tony, Jr. was bestowed upon Mix's old friend, veteran character actor Chill Wills.

Hoot Gibson was another favorite of the old Westerns who took a shine to Quarter Horses. He often rode a little palomino stallion named Goldie, until the horse was killed while performing a dangerous screen stunt. Gibson stuck with Quarter Horses but never shared billing, as did other stars.

Johnny Mack Brown, the All-American football star, began his long Western career riding the fashionable white horse that seemed to characterize the earlier Western films. To break the mold of the typecast cowboy hero, Brown realized he would have to shed the white steed. As a replacement, he chose a pretty little palomino Quarter Horse named Rebel, who carried Brown through the longest running series of Western films produced by any of the stars.

John Wayne was a longtime advocate of the Quarter Horse. His favorite was Banner, a large sorrel horse owned by the Hudkins Brothers stables in Hollywood. Banner not only carried Wayne but also many other actors to early screen glory. It was John Wayne, though, who brought out the best Banner had to offer, and for fourteen years Wayne rode the horse in almost every Western he made. Banner can still be seen on TV reruns such as "The Angel and the Badman," "The Fighting Kentuckians," "Fort Apache," and "Rio Bravo." Banner is best remembered as Wayne's mount in *Red River*. It just seemed natural for the horse to appear in the re-creation of the first cattle drive on the Chisholm Trail.

Quietness and dependability are essential qualities for a screen horse. On the sets where microphones and klieg lights are blaring and glaring, a horse can easily become frightened. The horse chosen by Wayne for the filming of *True Grit* was seven-eighths Thoroughbred and had all the outward characteristics of the breed; his highstrung nature could not adapt to the chaos around him. Barely into production, Wayne realized his mistake and switched to an almost identical sorrel gelding, a Quarter Horse named Dollar. Subsequently, Wayne used Dollar again in the sequel to *True Grit*, *Rooster Cogburn*.

Joel McCrea, undoubtedly one of the best horsemen in Hollywood, used Steel in a number of his pictures. But when Steel was not available, McCrea opted to feature his own personal mount, Dollar, the same flashy, blaze-faced Quarter Horse that was later used by John Wayne. Dollar derived his name from a distinctive white spot on his left hip that was the exact size of a silver dollar. Dollar carried his master through such McCrea epics as *Stranger on Horseback*, *Wichita*, *The Outriders*, and *Saddle Tramp*. In all, Dollar performed in about twenty McCrea Westerns.

Tim Holt, the action hero for RKO Studios, had begun his career by riding an American Saddlebred in his early pictures. But he too switched to the dependable Quarter Horse after World War II, and became so enamored that he set up a successful breeding program of his own. Holt then featured many of his palomino Quarter Horses in his films. Each was named Lightning. When the Western film lost its appeal, many of the stars went into retirement. Tim Holt moved to Oklahoma where he continued his lucrative hobby of breeding polled Hereford cattle and registered Quarter Horses. He was also an avid polo player.

Early television was literally saturated with Western programs. One of the top shows featured Dale Robertson in "Tales of Wells Fargo." For the action sequences, Robertson chose a sorrel Quarter Horse, Leo Jr., by Leo. When the program went from black and white into color production and was extended to an hour-long show, Robertson brought in a gray Quarter Horse gelding which he rode until the series was canceled.

Robertson's next TV venture was a series called "The Iron Horse." Again he used the Quarter Horse, a handsome black gelding named Hannibal. Robertson's affinity for the breed is natural, as he has successfully raised many fine Quarter Horses.

It's easy to understand why America's horse was the logical choice of the top screen cowboys. The films in which they appeared relied upon heavy action, instant bursts of quick speed, sliding stops, easy rollbacks, and a trusty disposition. And, on top of all that, the Quarter Horse could even make the star look better than he was!

Greenhorn Horse Traders

During my teenage years, I used to gallop horses in the summer months with visions of becoming a race rider. Even though my dad was a show horse trainer, I got up with the dawn and took out several sets before returning to the home barn to pursue reining and jumping work. Those were the days of meal tickets at the local cafe and movie-pal-night on Wednesdays, when two got in for the price of one.

The place of my employment was the Marwyck Ranch, owned by Barbara Stanwyck and Groucho Marx. In those days just about everyone in Hollywood was somehow connected with horses. Barbara Stanwyck was married to Robert Taylor at that time, and he had several show horses in training with the legendary M. R. Valdez. Every morning I saw Mrs. Taylor and every weekend the Mister.

After a stint in the Navy, my boyish figure had outgrown the ability to be a jockey. So I settled down in the arena, which became my only home. When Val retired, Bob brought his horses to me and, because of our long friendship, wanted to help me get a leg-up in the horse training business. Subsequently I acquired many Hollywood stars as clients and began building a business of my own.

A big part of making a living showing horses was through private sales to people who hopefully would keep the horse in training with me. In those days we didn't talk about marketing or networking, just buying and selling and how to do both with the greatest return. This is where Bob came in handy.

However, I must preempt with a little Hollywood gossip at this point. Barbara Stanwyck and Groucho Marx had long ago sold Marwyck (which became Northridge Farms, a famous racing stable). Barbara had been divorced from Bob, and Bob was now married to Ursula Theiss and lived not far from me in Mandeville Canyon, about a fifteen-minute drive.

Bob and I had put together a surefire plan, which worked like magic. If I had a potential client interested in buying a horse but I couldn't quite close the deal, I'd pick a time toward the end of the day for them to come one more time to "try the horse." Bob and I had a prearranged signal whereby he would call at a specified time and inquire how the transaction was coming along. I, in turn (if I needed his help), would ask my customers if they were in a hurry.

It went something like this: I would tell Bob to hold the line and then would say to my customer, "One of my clients, Mr. Robert Taylor, you know, the movie actor, is on the line and we need to talk a little. Do you mind?" Ninety-nine percent of the time they would reply, "No hurry, take your time."

Bob and I would chat about this and that and at the appropriate time, I would put my hand over the phone and ask my prospective buyers if they would like to accompany my wife and me to Robert Taylor's house for dinner. I would convey to them that my conversation with Mr. Taylor was going to take longer than expected and we could talk about our deal on the way over and back.

No one ever turned down an invitation to dine at Robert Taylor's house, especially with Ursula fixing her famous stuffed grape leaves. Of course the conversation on the drive over centered on my friendship with Bob, the other movie stars with horses in my barn, and my buyer's apparent concern over being properly dressed. Most were nervous and excited, growing more so the closer we got to Bob's house.

Bob was always the perfect host, welcoming them to his home and asking what brought them to the Don Burt training stable. He said all the right things: "Oh yes, I know the horse you're interested in, great horse; great place to ride and show out of; oh yes, I spend quite a bit of time there; I have four at the moment; yes, Don found every one for me; wouldn't go anywhere else." He was charming, and of course the dinner was delightful as always.

During the after-dinner conversation, Bob would ask if we could be excused so he and I could have a private chat. We'd retire to his office and let Ursula have the floor. Upon closing the door, a grinning Bob would anxiously ask, "How're we doing? How're we doing? Think we got a sale, partner?" I'd assure him that I thought we had us a sale. We would conclude our time in private and adjourn for the evening.

With my charges safely in tow, we'd proceed back to my place to continue the business at hand—selling a horse. Naturally the conversation on the way home always centered on how fantastic Mr. Taylor was; a regular guy not affected by his star status (one of the many things that made him special). And, yes, I sold the horse.

One time, though, we almost had to call the paramedics because a lady became so excited when Bob opened the door and reached for her hand that she fainted. We had to take her in and lay her down to revive her. She never was able to speak, just gasped and broke out in a cold sweat every time Bob got near her. We ended up having to leave without dinner, conversation, or selling a horse.

Another, when greeted with an extended hand, simply brushed it aside and planted a big kiss right on the lips of a very stunned movie star. Some started chattering incessantly, gushing out every word. The men would in turn stare at the beautiful actress serving them food and drink. Bob thought we should work out a plan or signal or something to prepare him for the unexpected. I tried to brief them on the way over but it's hard to predict the instant reaction many people have when coming face to face with a celebrity.

Bob and Ursula would take it all in stride; after all, they were helping a young horse trainer sell a horse. We even joked about how we rarely failed in our partnership (which I attribute to Bob's tutelage about business; he advised me to be honest and above board with all clients). I even made a deal with him that there was a money-back guarantee or trade-for-another on any horse deal in which he took part.

It taught me a great lesson and I never had the need to give a refund or replace any horse with which we dealt. Thinking back, we had some fun times and wild experiences as a couple of greenhorn horse traders.

Jocko: A Stuntman
On and Off the Set

While watching the Academy Awards in 1999, I was quite impressed with the segment that showed a brief collage of film clips because it included so many Western stars of yesterday. The only disappointment was not catching a glimpse of one of my good friends in any of the flashbacks. He played the Range Rider, Yancy Derringer, and even Tarzan. To me, he was one of the greatest stuntmen of all time who continued on into stardom.

Jock O'Mahoney (shortened to Mahoney) and I became friends when he lived about three blocks from my dad's stable in Burbank. He came to ride and practice nearly every day and would often cart me with him to the movie set, where he excelled at his craft. I've seen him stand flat-footed and jump up like a coiled spring, clearing one horse and landing astride the one next to it. I was in awe of this great athlete.

He was a swimming, basketball, and football phenomenon for the University of Iowa. Later he served for nine years as a member of the board of directors for the Screen Actors Guild. In 1984, "Jocko" was honored with the Stuntmen's Life Achievement Award, which included a film salute to his many accomplishments in the movie and television industry.

All through my years as a horse trainer, Jocko was always there. He'd go to shows with me, grooming and riding, just to help out. Later in life, his 6-foot-5-inch-plus frame broadened, and he nurtured a character actor's beard to complement his graying sideburns. His burly individuality was only a front for the many kindnesses he bestowed upon my wife and me.

One time when we were at a horse show, I was looking for my

wife. Not having any success, I yelled at Jocko who was leaning on the rail. "Have you seen Ardy?" He turned his head and answered, "Sure have." With that, my wife popped her head around from in front of Jocko and both belly laughed at their deception.

Great friends are few, and when I was gone a lot judging or conducting seminars, Jocko would call Ardy on the phone every day just to see if she needed anything. He was that kind of a guy.

In his earlier performing years, he was a grueling taskmaster. His backyard had an abundance of jungle gym equipment and a huge pool to help keep him in shape. He not only kept himself in condition, but put his family through the same regimen as well. His stepdaughter, Academy Award-winning actress Sally Field, and his own daughter, Princess, had a routine mapped out for them everyday, mostly under water, diving and swimming endless laps in the pool.

Discipline was his trademark and he always did his own stunts. Once, while filming *Tarzan Goes to India*, he and another great stuntman, actor Woody Strode, were scripted to fight to the death. Jocko had a fever of over 102 degrees, but the show went on. Their combat has become one of the greatest fight scenes ever filmed.

Jocko was a gifted storyteller and a quick wit. We spent many an evening listening to his tales of riding elephants, talking to chimpanzees, and chasing bad guys. One incident I'll never forget happened when I was just starting out training horses and Jocko was going to "help" me. I was to gentle this particular horse so it could handle any situation, especially out on the trail in the wild. The plan was that Jocko would try to spook the horse at various places along the way. I'd do the riding and he'd come up with all sorts of paraphernalia so the horse would get used to anything and everything that might occur unexpectedly.

Well, the plan not only got us both bucked off but nearly killed. I was riding along a narrow trail not far from the barn. Jocko had somehow found an old bearskin rug and was hiding behind a huge oak tree with this rug covering his entire body. He was real soft moving and I didn't hear him come up behind me at a trot. He did a hind crouper vault and landed behind me on the horse. Naturally the horse broke in two, flinging me, Jocko, and the bearskin rug high in the air. We all hit the ground one on top of the other—me, Jocko, and the bear hide, in that order. When we discovered we were all right, Jocko said, "Do you realize we would have been paid a couple of thousand for that stunt if the cameras had been rolling?"

When Jock Mahoney left us, his friends threw the biggest Irish wake I've ever attended. They rented a large hall and the list of those who paid tribute looked like the audience at the Oscars. Stars of today and those who had retired made the party a Who's Who of Hollywood.

After a night of toasts and remembrances, a memorial service was held the following day at a chapel high in the Santa Monica hills. For a final send-off, we said our goodbyes and a single balloon was released into the sky by Jocko's wife, Autumn. The balloon rose to about fifty feet and circled overhead for about fifteen minutes, as if it were saying goodbye. Then it ascended to about a hundred feet and tarried for another ten minutes or so. We all craned our necks as the balloon did a final bob and weave. The tail actually appeared to be waving to us as it spun with great speed into the wild blue yonder.

Every time I see an old Western on TV, it's easy to pick out the stunts that were done by Jocko, such as jumping off of balconies or from trees, riding off a cliff, or jumping burning wagons. He was one of the best and it was only natural he went on to be a star in the acting department.

114

Wild Bill Elliott

If you were a horse trainer during the fifties and sixties—in southern California, anyway—you lived a diverse and exciting lifestyle. Most trainers showed every kind of horse imaginable (I even had a world champion 3-gaited horse and a world champion fine harness horse). Some worked part-time on the rodeo circuit or, if they happened to live in the Hollywood area, doubled for famous movie stars. You even played polo when a substitute was needed, and rode steeplechase races at Del Mar to encourage that sport. But with all the rip-roaring experiences, it's the people you met along the way that you remember.

At a 1997 American Horse Council convention, several attendees wanted to know how well I knew Wild Bill Elliott (probably because I've touched on him in previous columns). I recounted how Bill Elliott had willed his saddle to me before he died, but circumstances allowed it to sit in an old friend's garage for many years. When I finally took possession, the famous saddle with "B. E." carved on the horn reminded me that he was not just a star but also a true horseman.

Back then there was an entire era built on the "B" Westerns, with heroes like Tom Mix, Buck Jones, and Tim McCoy, to name a few. But it was a movie serial based on the adventures of Wild Bill Hickock that took this matinee idol to fame. The fringed leather shirt, big black hat, and twin bone-handled Colts were his familiar trademarks. He wore his guns in reverse style to most Western heroes, but it didn't slow his draw.

The serial was a box-office smash with audiences returning religiously to the theatre, not to view the main feature, but to see what happened next to "Wild Bill." His first name was quickly changed

115

to Wild Bill by his fans and the studio was elated. They promptly issued a second serial followed by a third series. He turned out over fifty live-action pictures, which put him on top of the heap.

However, in the late 30s, the singing cowboy erupted on the screen and many action stars fell out of favor. But Wild Bill went right on grinding out the slam-bang action pictures he was famous for, without crooning a note in any of them.

Then, in the 40s, Republic Studios picked up Elliott for an eight-picture series. These movies were some of the best he ever made. Following that, he was cast in the Red Ryder series of sixteen pictures. Once again it allowed him to play Wild Bill in his own inimitable way and boosted his popularity even more with the fans.

The head of Republic decided it was time to upgrade the studio image and changed the "Wild Bill" to plain "William" and cast Elliott in a series of big-budget films. Despite the loss of action and poor scripts, they were good Elliott vehicles and he prospered from them.

It is understandable why Elliott enjoyed a career that spanned some twenty years as a top cowboy movie star. He was a natural— an excellent horseman who delivered the action and his lines well, was fast on the draw, and had a pleasing personality.

His real name was Gordon Elliott, and he was born in 1903 in Pattonsburg, Missouri. He grew up in Kansas City where his father ran the stockyards, which gave him an early exposure to horses and real-life cowboys. Being raised with an appreciation for horses and the land, he was always well-mounted on-screen and off. For the upgraded Republic pictures, he purchased a gray Quarter Horse stud named Stormy Day Moore from the Waggoner Ranch in Texas. Stormy was one of the best-looking horses to ever enjoy a screen career, and was perfect in size and conformation for Bill's lanky form.

Away from the cameras, Bill was a real-life cowboy and rancher, raising Herefords and Quarter Horses. He was an enthusiastic cutting horse fan as well. In 1950 Bill Elliott purchased a good cutting horse called Red Boy from Lloyd Jenkins of Fort Worth. The horse carried the National Cutting Horse Association certificate of ability No. 47 and was registered under the AQHA No. 15810, which identified him as Ray Boy by Billy by King P-234, out of a Swenson Ranch mare. Bill campaigned Red Boy successfully until he sold the horse in 1956. The gelding went on to earn $20,000 in NCHA-approved shows. It was also about that time I started training "Baldy" (Bill's personal appearance horse that became my car-jumping mount), which he had sold to the president of the Squirt Company. Bill was a longtime member of the NCHA and in 1952 served on the Executive Committee.

Bill owned ranches in Calabassas, California and in Las Vegas, Nevada, in addition to his sprawling home in Brentwood. At the Brentwood home he had an elaborately furnished workshop where he spent many hours of relaxation. He was a fine craftsman and his hobby was making pistol handles from various exotic materials such as jade, ivory, and rosewood. Bill went into retirement in the late 50s, and his cowboy career came to an end in 1965 after a long bout with cancer.

I first met Wild Bill when I was asked by the studio to teach one of the "Little Beavers" to ride for the Red Ryder series. Bill came by to watch and it wasn't long before we started riding together. I was also schooling some trick-riding horses for a girl who did a lot of doubling on the set. He was interested in all aspects of horse training and put his knowledge to use on the screen. He could really ride. Come to think of it, he probably could have become a horse trainer—but he made it big anyway!

The Golden Boot

The River Bottom was famous to horse people long before "beautiful downtown Burbank" was made a household phrase by Johnny Carson. Even though I've written much about this little strip of land nestled alongside the Los Angeles River, requests keep piling up for more history.

One of the most significant products generated from this area was the people. Those who grew up there or used it as a layover or watering hole have maintained a lifelong camaraderie. Many to this day stay in touch, from trainers, movie stars, and jockeys to business tycoons and champion cowboys. Horses, movies, and industry have a shared lifestyle, a common thread woven between glamour and nostalgia. So, when "one of us" is honored in any way, we become an even tighter family when sharing the good news.

Eighteen years ago, veteran sidekick Pat Buttram conceived the notion for a special award to be given not only to our cowboy stars but also to the writers, directors, character actors, and stunt people who have contributed to the Western tradition in film and television. Since Pat's first presentation to Bob Steele of a fancy belt buckle embellished with a golden boot, the idea has grown into a gala celebration. Famous names and faces have gathered annually to honor the Westerners who have so indelibly become part of an American tradition.

In 2000, when Donna Hall Fishburn was notified she was to receive the prestigious "Golden Boot Award," it was time once again to relive the glory days gone by. Being one of only three stunt-women so honored in the last seventeen years, Donna was quite surprised. But from her early days riding show horses through her career as a famous trick rider, she has rightfully earned the award.

She was always at home in the arena or on the movie set—anywhere horses were featured.

A trick rider since her preteen years and the daughter of jockey Frank "Shorty" Hall, Donna was prepared for a life of everyday risk taking. She had her first taste of trick riding at the age of three when her dad put her on a horse. Being too small to grip the animal when it bolted beside a fence, she got hung upside down in the stirrups. Dad set her back in the saddle again and Donna rode her mount—she has never been afraid of any horse since. By seven she owned her own horse and at eight she was showing jumping horses.

Trick riding came naturally. Donna performed her daredevil stunts in rodeos, and doubled for actors in movies and on television. Rodeo veteran Casey Tibbs was so impressed that he invited her to perform at both Madison Square Garden and Boston Garden. In her spare time on the set, she would give riding lessons to the stars who couldn't pass muster on the horsebacking requirement . . . which even included Tom Selleck.

She is one of the few women in the history of motion pictures and TV to have driven and chased 4- and 6-horse teams. However, she once told me, the transfers were the toughest. To gallop beside a train moving at twenty-five miles per hour, bring the horse alongside the engine, and then escape from the saddle to the train is difficult. You all have probably seen her doing the same transfer to a galloping stagecoach. Donna did a lot of the planning on these sequences, working up stunts to match the dialog.

Another tough one is jumping from a stagecoach seat to the wagon tongue in the midst of a team of four horses tearing along at full speed, grabbing the reins, and bringing the team to a halt.

Donna performed stunts on about eighty-five of the half-hour segments of the Annie Oakley series on television, including all the opening and stock shots.

In addition to doing horse stunts, in which, she claims, "everything is up to the horse," she has played other risky roles in movies. She has fallen down stairs, been hit by trucks, and ridden in cars being chased around curves on one wheel by police cars. But horses, she insists, are her favorite props.

To list but a few of the other TV shows that engaged her stunting talents: *Have Gun Will Travel, Wanted Dead or Alive, The Lone Ranger, The Virginian,* and *Laramie.* Some movies you may have seen Donna in include *Cat Ballou, Cheyenne Autumn,* and *How The West Was Won.* In the latter, Donna doubled another Burbank native and school chum of mine, Debbie Reynolds.

She jokes that the closest she ever came to winning an Academy Award was owning the horse that Doris Day sang to in *Calamity Jane.* Doris took home the Oscar; Donna took all the risks . . . such as running along the top of a moving train and riding upside down on a galloping horse.

During her rodeo days, she went from queen to Roman riding to drags and vaults—and that was mostly for fun. Her scrapbook of photos and memories gives a true history of the horse in Hollywood—making a horse fall in a river, hustling a runaway, pulling a horse over backwards, chasm jumping. The book is full of written accolades from stars, both past and present, to one of the most modest and unassuming giants of the horse world.

From all across the country, famous names have been honored here in a tribute to the "Western." To much of the world, the legend of the American West embodies America herself. I'm proud to say Donna Hall is one of my longtime best friends and she joins an impressive list of recipients of this award, among them Ronald Reagan, John Wayne, Roy Rogers, Dale Evans, Gene Autry, and Ben Johnson, to name just a few.

Hooray For Hollywood

"**H**ooray for Hollywood, that screwy, ballyhooey Hollywood . . . where any office boy or young mechanic can be a panic with just a good looking pan..." Those words to an old song lured many a wannabe to the tinsel town famous for turning unknowns into overnight stars.

The other day I had a call from Frank Stallone. "Hey, buddy," he said. "Are you going to the Golden Boot Awards?"

"It's not that time of year already, is it?" I asked, remembering the invitation sitting on my desk.

"It sure is . . . this Saturday night," he reminded me.

I've written about the Golden Boot Awards as a way to recognize the achievements of those who had significant involvement in the Western film and TV industry.

Since its inception, the idea has taken off and has outgrown each of its many venues. The buckle has been replaced with an actual golden boot, reminiscent of the Oscar statue. As the ceremony gained in popularity, it has mushroomed into a gala celebrity function where now you can rub elbows with all the Hollywood Cowboys, whether in front of or behind the camera, retired or a fledgling.

In fact, after we built the Los Angeles Equestrian Center, the festivities graduated to that facility in 1987. I even remember who received the awards that year, which is a feat in itself. On stage were Gene Barry, Harry Carey, Jr., Andre de Toth, Richard Farnsworth, Rhonda Fleming, Glenn Ford, Robert Livingston, Joel McCrea, Debra Paget, John Russell, Woody Strode and, (posthumously), Tom Mix. I had actually ridden with Richard Farnsworth, Joel McCrea, and Woody Strode, and two other stars,

Jock Mahoney and Ben Johnson (who were previous recipients), just the day before.

We rode out on the trail for a while, then Jocko and I decided to go on up into the hills of Griffith Park, something we did quite often. We rode across the legendary swinging bridge that spans the Los Angeles River, through the tunnel that goes under the freeway, and into the Park's hills. The trail we took circles the Forest Lawn Cemetery that was once Hudkin's Ranch, home to many a Western movie location. Jocko, one of the Hollywood greats in the stunt business before becoming a star himself, kept pointing out places where some of his favorite stunts were performed. Jumping out of a tree onto a stagecoach, the countless chases across the valley, bull-dogging the bad guys off their horses—these were all things I was familiar with. This was mainly because as a young'un I rode match races there nearly every Sunday and drove the haywagon full of kids out on a Saturday night date.

But I guess that's what the Golden Boot night is all about—memories of Westerns gone by and the promise of those to come. We stopped up on top to rest and took in the view. He said to me, "Just think of all the cowboys who worked in the picture business; most of them are resting right down there." We rode back and joined up with the others for a night of merriment and reminiscing right in the center of the Equestrian Center's arena.

In 2001, in addition to the honorees, there was the Centennial Award memorializing Clark Gable's 100th birthday. This was the reason for Frank's call. He was attending with Clark Gable's son, John Clark Gable, and wanted my wife and me to get together with them.

The honors took on an even greater meaning for me personally because of one recipient. Set to receive an award, along with Alex

Cord (who still plays polo at the Equestrian Center), Chuck Norris, Andrew Prine, and Eli Wallach, was Loren Janes, a longtime friend and one of (if not) the greatest stuntmen of more recent times. Loren became a professional movie and TV stuntman and stunt coordinator in the early 50s by making an 80-foot dive from a cliff on Catalina Island. Since then he has doubled nearly every major star and worked in over five hundred films doing a lot more than just riding horses. He and I go way back—over forty years—when he was on the Olympic Pentathlon Team and I was his riding coach for two Olympic Games. When I met him, even though he grew up on a working cattle ranch, he always went through gates to get to the other side of the fence. It was my job to have him jump over fences at a full gallop cross-country.

Dale Robertson, another great star and breeder of Quarter Horses, was again tapped to be the master of ceremonies. He can make you laugh just by reading the menu. This year's shindig was held at Merv Griffin's Beverly Hilton Hotel in the heart of Beverly Hills, which is a long way from the small gathering at a local restaurant. Every year the banquet gets bigger, and now includes a silent auction. It seems everybody wants to be a cowboy.

The talk of the evening naturally centered on those being honored with awards, but there also was the buzz among everyone assembled that "we need more great Westerns." Everyone raised their glasses in accordance!

Boots and Saddles

Most people spend a lot of time preparing for the change in seasons, especially for spring and winter. In southern California we don't do much changing except maybe for the type of jacket or boots we wear.

The other day I was in the process of finding my winter boots (which differ only from my summer boots in that they have rain stains and old mud-caked lines) and discovered I have a closet full of old boots. I find it hard to throw away a good, old, comfortable pair of boots. They just keep piling up because I'm sure I'll wear them again someday.

My dilemma and the reason for all this sorting out is because the AQHA Executive Committee is going on a ride in the Palo Duro Canyon. Since spending a great deal of time in Texas, I've become quite fascinated with the life of the Comanche Indians and particularly the history of Quanah Parker. The Comanches were reputed to be the greatest of all Indian horsemen and capturing them was only accomplished by getting rid of their horses and putting them afoot. Then, watching "Lonesome Dove" on TV and reading the story of Charlie Goodnight piqued my interest in the Palo Duro and the great cattle drives of history.

This, of course, has nothing to do with my collection of old boots except that I needed a pair, not too new or too old but broken-in just right, to maintain my image as a trail rider. My Wranglers should be just a little faded; spurs, with a touch of rust; chaps, I would leave at home; shirt, soft and comfortable with a wrinkle here and there; and my hat needed a trace of sweat around the band. Packing was going to be no problem, as all this special attire could be put in one bag.

Now I ride a lot with little regard to my persona but history demands the research and comfort that makes one feel part of the era. Comfort was, in those days, a cherished thing as opposed to all of the accoutrements deemed necessary for life today, especially horse show life. We must have the latest, most modern, and definitely in-style article of clothing along with the ultimate in silver mountings for the halter, saddle, and bridle. When the styles change, we head for the local tack shop and bring happiness to the owner and equipment manufacturers.

This simple, several-hour trail ride over the true paths of history monopolized most of my time for days. It even drew a few smirks from my wife as I laid out, discarded, and settled on the items, only to change them the next day. But undaunted, I continued in my quest for the perfect outfit to ride the Indian trails of yesteryear.

A few nights later we had an old-time (even older than me) rancher friend over for dinner. Our conversation eventually shifted to tack and attire and he said, "Do you know why winter boots are more comfortable than summer ones?" Not sure if he was right or wrong, I said, "No." "Because you get your winter boots wet and wear them dry and then they naturally mold to your feet," he answered; he went on, "Let's go to the tack room so I can see your saddles."

We adjourned to my office where I kept them. "Know why a cowboy never parts with his favorite saddle?" he asked, and then answered: "When you find a saddle that fits like a glove and you can ride it all day and half the night, seven days a week, you never can give it up. In fact, Indians today who cowboy in New Mexico pawn their saddles in winter and reclaim them in summer, but never sell them. They let someone else keep it safe when they're not using it and it gives them a few bucks besides."

"Used to be," he went on, "We'd buy a new saddle, take it to the ranch, throw it in the water trough, soak it good, and then ride it dry. Fits a man's body that way." He broke out in a wide grin, chuckling as he said, "Can you see one of those guys today taking a new saddle all covered with silver and deliberately throwing it in the water trough? I'll guarantee if you took one of their saddles and did that to it, they'd not only have a heart attack but probably string you up on the spot."

"Now here's the best saddle you've got," he said, picking out an oldie but goody. "This one's had some use."

"Yeah," I said, "My favorite, and it has a story all its own." I proceeded to tell it:

"I once rode some horses for a Western star named Wild Bill Elliott. There's his 'B. E.' carved right on the horn. He rode this saddle in many movies as Red Ryder and other characters. He also did a lot of cutting and was a real cowboy, not just in Hollywood. He let me use it at shows when I didn't have enough saddles to go around. In fact, the year I won five championships at the Cow Palace, two were with jumping horses but the others were ridden with this saddle.

"Well, as Hollywood goes, popularity went on to other stars and Wild Bill kind of faded from sight. We kept in touch for awhile, then lost track until I heard he had died.

"About fifteen or twenty years went by, and then a lady called me one night and wanted to know if I was the horse trainer who used to train Bill Elliott's horses. I told her I was, and she said she had something she thought belonged to me. Seems she took care of Bill in his last years and when he died he had willed his saddle to me. The lady had no idea how or where to find me until she saw my name in a horse magazine. She tracked me down and gave me this saddle that had been in her garage all those years. Of course it's one of my prized possessions."

As we bade goodnight, my rancher friend turned and said, "He probably threw it in the water trough and rode it dry; looks like it's got a good seat and a great ride."

HORSES
AND
HORSEMEN

Baldy

While I was off traveling one year, my wife decided to completely redo my office and appropriately renamed it my "retreat." She has made it so comfortable with all my memorabilia, plus a TV, wet bar, and fireplace, that if I didn't know better, I'd think she might be trying to run me out of the house. I've always admired Will Rogers's rustic ranch house and now I have a cowboy retreat of my own. It's a great place to reflect on the future and relive the bygone days.

When we were sorting through all the old trophies, buckles, saddles, scrapbooks, and pictures, we came upon one picture, actually a newspaper clipping, of "Baldy" and me jumping over cars. Yup, in my younger days I was a little unbridled, which caused me to jump a horse over a car or two when the pay was right.

It just so happened that at the 1950s reunion last year, one of the testimonials was dedicated to the great jumping horses of that era. "Baldy," being the Pacific Coast Horse Shows Association Jumper Champion a couple of years in a row, was therefore featured in the speech, which in turn reminded everyone of his prowess outside of the show ring.

Baldy was a Quarter Horse. However, his papers were lost somewhere in his earlier career as Wild Bill Elliott's rearing horse. Baldy was also the horse Elliot rode consistently when leading the grand entry for Tommy Steiner's Rodeo Company in the early fifties.

Shortly after that, Baldy was bought by the owners of the Squirt Company for their daughter to ride in Western Horsemanship and Stock Horse classes. They had the horse in training with me for about a year when an extraordinary occurrence took place.

One day I had him turned out in my bullpen, which had solid, six-foot walls without any "look-out" area. I had just opened the door to take him out when a fire engine roared by under full siren with whistles and bells clanging. I stared in disbelief as the horse, spooked by the clamor, jumped over the wall from a completely flat-footed stance. At best he was a mediocre stock horse, but with this turn of events, the path of Baldy's new career was brightly lit. It wasn't three weeks later that he won his first big open jumper stake.

In those days they had "rub classes," which were judged by touches as well as knockdowns and refusals. Because there was no time taken then, they would just keep raising the jumps to break the ties. Baldy was a horse that you had to keep taking back, almost canter in place, until about three strides away from the fence. Then, I would urge and he would explode into the air. It was a little like riding a rocket and I remember it was a lot of fun at the time.

Also way back then, they would set a course of all five-foot jumps with no ground lines. Slip fillets (thin laths) were placed on top of the highest rail and if moved by the horse's front legs or feet, it was scored as one fault; if moved by the hind feet it rendered a one-half fault. A front knockdown was scored four faults and a hind knockdown, two faults.

Baldy was a master at not wanting to touch anything. This especially came in handy when jumping over cars. He had one problem, though, that was also remembered. He had been taught to rear on cue (from his Hollywood days), so I had to be extra careful not to ask him to rear while heading for a fence or any other jump-able obstacle. It was pretty spectacular, as I was reminded at the reunion, to see Baldy jump a car, stop and rear, walk a few steps on his hind legs, and then exit.

One of my fondest memories of showing Baldy was at the Cow Palace's Big Jump (they didn't call it a Grand Prix in those days). I was tied for the championship with Barbara Worth and her horse Balbriggan, who was close to eighteen hands. Barbara Worth Oakford is a world famous horsewoman and show jumping hall-of-famer who, incidentally, has shown every kind of horse imaginable, and rode Poco Lena to her first three blue ribbons in cutting.

She had gone first in the jump-off and finished with a score of a ½ fault for a hind rub. I had jumped eleven of the twelve fences, all clean, and was heading down to the last five-foot, single pole with no ground line. I changed my mind a thousand times on the way to that fence. Too slow, too fast, take back once more, no, just right, too close—it seemed like an eternity getting there. Then Baldy blasted off into the air. He was a little close and jumped off to the left. While in midair at the top of his crest, I looked left at the arena wall and right smack into the face of a woman spectator who was seated in the first row box and had leaned over the rail for a better view. We were so close I probably could have kissed her. However, that wasn't in the cards because she screamed and fell back into the box seat, scattering people and things as she tumbled. I'm not quite sure if that's what made Baldy give an extra surge at that moment or if he just didn't want to be beaten, but he trued his course, jumped about a foot over the pole, and we walked away with the championship.

River Bottom Heyday

A while back, AQHA's past president, Howard Weiss, invited me to be the after-dinner speaker at the Saddle and Sirloin, one of the oldest, strictly riding and roping clubs in the Los Angeles area. Shortly after my engagement there, I received an invitation to be the breakfast speaker at the prestigious Jonathan Club, one of the last "businessmen only" clubs in L.A. to finally yield to female members. My topic on both occasions was the horse business around Los Angeles, and more explicitly, the history of the River Bottom.

At one time, this area of Burbank was the focal point and home to nearly all of the famous horses and horsemen from the 1930s on. My family bought their first stable there when I was about five or six years old. It was nestled in between George Kennedy's (Clyde's dad) barn and that of Jimmy Williams's relatives. During that time, there was a real estate development called Riverside Ranchos. If you bought a house, they gave you a horse, and to this day, instead of garages or swimming pools, there is a stable in every backyard on a lot consisting of 50 x 100 feet. As Johnny Carson would say, "Only in Burbank."

One thing each audience wanted to know about was the famous swinging bridge (which, by the way, is still used today). The bridge spans the L.A. River and is the only access to the trails of Griffith Park. This suspension bridge of approximately four feet wide by 150 feet long has carried hundreds of horses each week to the wide open areas between Burbank and downtown Los Angeles.

I used to ride across that bridge even before I was seven years old and vividly remember my first encounter. My dad took me along to explore the crossing and the trails we could take clients on. We started across the bridge, my dad in the lead, and about halfway across, as the bridge started to swing, my old pony stopped dead in his tracks. I spurred and kicked in an effort to make him go, but he wouldn't budge. My dad, who was already across, began to give me instructions. Nothing worked. Finally, in desperation, I spurred in remote areas (anywhere my legs could reach) but was only rewarded with my mount kneeling and bowing. After I got him up, I proceeded with more persuasion only to succeed in making him sit down. My dad finally came to my rescue. Not only was this my first experience with a swinging bridge, but with a trained trick pony as well.

In those days the River Bottom housed many famous horses and horsemen and became the learning area and watering hole for lots of the Hollywood stars of the era—especially those who made Westerns. I rode across that bridge for many years with Jocko Mahoney (The Range Rider), Wild Bill Elliott (Red Ryder and the one whose saddle I still ride today), Hoot Gibson (who had a club called The Painted Post Saloon), and Jerry Ambler (champion bronc rider who owned the Amble Inn). Tim McCoy used to head groups at the crossing into Griffith Park and trick ropers Sam Garrett and Montie Montana were regulars. I rode across with Casey Tibbs, Bud and Bill Linderman, and Wallace Brooks on the way to Hudkins Ranch where lots of Westerns were made and match races were held nearly every Sunday afternoon.

Even after I moved away and had clients like Robert Taylor and Clark Gable, I still hauled back frequently to take them riding on the trails of Griffith Park. We would ride to the ridge overlooking Hollywood and the freeway, which was once only a road with a bridle trail alongside.

The bridge got quite a reputation with trainers of the day. They would pony horses across the bridge and when one would go willingly, he was passed off as broke. While in my teens, I used the swinging bridge in other ways. As I always had horses to train, I spent a lot of time crossing back and forth. More often than not I would meet a damsel in distress trying to get from one side to the other. I, being cavalier, would offer my services and on several occasions rode double, telling her to hang on to me tightly as I schooled her horse. Ah yes, yesterday was great fun at the River Bottom.

There was also tragedy when the Pickwick Stable burned down destroying more than twenty horses. However, it was rebuilt again to house many champions. The area also contained Ficketts Corner, a ride-a-while stables that, together with the Horse Palace on down the river, was home to nearly all the horse shows held in the greater Los Angeles area. I even used to hire out at the railroad yard to unload the show horses shipped there by rail.

In fact, it was at a show held in the Horse Palace (formerly known as McLaughlin Stadium, built by the late Victor McLaughlin for his light horse troop) where a cattle buyer from the east met up with Clyde Kennedy and Barbara Worth. He succumbed to the life of a horse trainer after being introduced to the blue ribbon-winning stock horse named Spook. That now famous trainer and Hall-of-Famer, Don Dodge, walked into the River Bottom one way and rode out another.

Even today, if you want to run into movie cowboys or those riding dude horses by the hour, as well as top-notch polo, saddle horse, hunter, jumper, Western pleasure, and reining horse trainers, they're still there side by side along Riverside Drive. And, on any given day, you'll probably have to wait in line to cross the legendary swinging bridge.

M. R. Valdez: A Legend

It's rare that my plane is ever early into the Dallas/Fort Worth airport. On one such occasion, I sauntered to my connecting gate and even had plenty of time to rendezvous with several horsemen who were joining me for a meeting in Amarillo. As you know, when horse folk get talkative, it usually centers on their equine talents (horse and human).

However, this conversation generated a different sentiment; a feeling of guilt because we don't pass on the talents of those gone before. Maybe it was the recent passing of Jimmy Williams that spurred our conscience. We all agreed that we turn horses out when we finish with them and do the same with great horsemen, rarely to be heard from again. We concurred on our need to perpetuate their knowledge and memory for future generations.

The tone of our powwow brought to mind an experience I had many years ago regarding this very subject. I'm sure everyone, at some time in his or her life, has had an idol. Mine just happened to be the greatest reinsman that ever lived. I would break out in goose bumps when the announcer would say, " . . . and ridden by M. R. Valdez." Valdez, as we have always referred to him, was a magic name; he was the "master." To watch him work or show a horse was like seeing an artist bring a canvas to life.

I was in Hawaii in the early seventies to judge a horse show when I came across the master. We (my wife, youngest daughter, and I) were on our way from the hotel to do some shopping. As we drove down the street I noticed a man walking his dogs by the beach. I glanced at him as we passed and made the comment, "If I didn't know better, I'd swear that was Valdez." I kept driving, trying to convince myself that it couldn't be my idol, as no one had heard about him for years.

My wife urged me to go back and as I approached the man, I got those same goose bumps again. "Val?" I said. His eyes sparkled as he looked up and answered, "Yes, I'm Valdez." We chatted and I made a date to come back and visit.

Even though I had known Val and Vivian Valdez for many years, I really didn't know much about his life before or after his show ring career. So, during our visit, I asked him to take me back to his earlier days.

"Well, Don," he said, "I'm ninety-three years old and I've saddled a lot of horses. I grew up in Presidio, Texas, and when I was about ten my father took over a large cow outfit in Mexico where I worked with cattle and horses for about seven years. After a lot of hard work and long hours, I decided I had learned enough. So, in 1899 I headed back to Texas and cowboyed my way into New Mexico and on into Colorado where I worked for a man who had two ranches (cattle and sheep). He also raised horses and I was hired to work the colts, until a Wild West show lured me away in about 1905.

"I traveled with the show a couple of years, riding bucking horses, until it went broke in Los Angeles. After about a year in L.A., I made my way back to Utah where I picked up my horse and saddle and went to work breaking horses. I was a range cowboy and remuda boss for years and then I came back to L.A. where I met my wife. We settled down and farmed a spell.

"But horses were definitely in my blood, and the horse shows were rolling right along then with many large stables. So, I took the job of managing a show stable belonging to Marco Hellman."

I interjected with my remembrance of when I first spoke to the "great Valdez." I was about twelve, showing in a junior stock horse class at "The Horse Palace" (today, it's the Golden State Freeway!). I saw Valdez watching me, so I decided to show him how good I was. I worked my horse on the rail, up and down, doubling back into the rail. My horse was really coming back fast into the fence. After a couple of dozen times, I rode over to the "master" and with all the confidence I could muster, I said, "How's that for a turning horse?" A slight smile grew on Val's face and he said to me, "Son, when you get him turning away from the rail as good as you've got him turning into the rail, then you'll have a reined horse." A lesson I've never forgotten.

Val never talked much in those days and now we were chattering like birds on a rail. You learned by watching him work, what he did and how he did it. He was a showman, a quiet gentleman who stole the show every time he entered the ring. Val had a unique style of his own, from the shape of his hat to the way he mounted his horse.

I finally got to my ultimate question: "What part of showing did you like most?"

"The rope work with the sack," he said, without hesitation. In those days, part of the stock horse routine—besides the figure eight, stop, and spin—was to "work the sack."

A gunnysack of sand was roped. The horse then ran back and forth turning squarely when the end of the rope was reached, during which time the rider would pass the rope over the horse's head and tail showing he was not rope shy. After several stops and turns showing the passing of the rope, he would then back up until the rope was taut (from saddle horn to sack), à la calf roping. The rider would then dismount, walk to the sack, and wait for the signal from the judge to return to the horse.

Val's inimitable style of dismounting, walking to the sack, standing with hands on his hips and looking only at the judge, never at the horse, gave the feeling of utmost confidence that the horse would never make a wrong move. A nod from the judge and the most famous Valdez trick of all, hopping into the stirrup (later imitated by every Hollywood cowboy hero), reunited the man and horse as a team.

We were all so engrossed in preserving the past that we almost missed our Amarillo flight. We hurried aboard, everyone jockeying for a chance to relate a story about a moment in time.

Ebony Night

While reminiscing with M. R. Valdez and putting together the stories about him, a name kept cropping up at every turn. Everyone I talked with about his career mentioned the famous stock horse Ebony Night. I can remember, as if it were yesterday, watching the black horse perform. In fact, I can't ever remember him not winning every class he entered. I called his owner, Roland Rich Woolley, a retired attorney, and told him I wanted to tell the story of the Thoroughbred gelding who, after winning races at Hollywood Park, became the nation's leading stock horse and a true legend in his own time. I made an appointment and saw Mr. Woolley at his office where we spent reflective hours looking at pictures, reliving the "good ol' days" of the horse show world.

On April 22, 1937, a mare named Vibrant gave birth to a foal by the Kentucky Derby winner Flying Ebony. As both Vibrant and Flying Ebony were black, it was only natural the foal would be black too, and so it was that misty morning on the Alisal Ranch in Santa Barbara. Ebony Night was the third foal of the mare, and being a half-brother to Cargador and King June, who were both winners at the track, considerable success was expected from this black foal. He was sold to Walter G. McCarty and, with the famous George Woolf in the saddle, galloped home a winner in his second start, which took place on June 27, 1939 at Hollywood Park.

A training accident set Ebony Night back somewhat, but still he went on with limited success. The next year he was given a vacation at Rolling Hills Ranch with the expectation of having his injuries healed by the time the Santa Anita meeting rolled around.

The horse was ready but the tragedy at Pearl Harbor on December 7th reared its ugly head and racing was forgotten until the world crisis was over. This forced Ebony Night, as well as many other horses, into retirement for a while; and that's when Roland Rich Woolley came into the picture, providing a complete change of pace for the horse.

Having grown up on a vast cattle ranch in Idaho, Woolley knew and appreciated good horses. In the fall of '42 while looking over the stock at Rolling Hills Ranch, Woolley spotted a sleek black colt (by now a four-year-old) and after only taking one look, he told Walt McCarty, "That just might make a superior stock horse." The ownership of Ebony Night was transferred that same day, and by evening the black Thoroughbred was embarking on a pathway to stardom in the show arena by arriving at the stable of M. R. Valdez, the best Western trainer anywhere.

Val immediately started the horse on the "Valdez system for training stock horses," which meant studying the horse for many days, scrutinizing his reactions, estimating his character, and gauging his temperament. Only after this had been done did he start to work the horse.

"Val teaches by repetition, going slowly, and being lenient; he is persistent but gentle," Woolley reminisced. "He avoids crowding or rushing a horse, which allows his charge to learn by putting him at the same task over and over, instilling each lesson into the animal's brain to a degree that it becomes automatic, or sort of a reflex. But with it all, he manages to make training pleasant for the horse." These words were spoken as Woolley looked out of the window, and I'm sure as he spoke, the vision of Val and Ebony Night working together was depicted in the clouds.

The black horse was put through a long schooling period and advanced steadily. Months passed before Val considered the former racehorse ready for public showing. He was entered in the sixth annual horse show of The Riviera Country Club in the fall of '45. Having won the class, Roland Rich Woolley was so elated that he entered him in the Marine Corps League Show the following week, and again he took home the "blue."

Winning became a way of life for both Ebony Night and Val. As we talked, the friendship between Woolley and Valdez was evident. He said, "You know, Val is realistic in his appraisal of a horse. He never allows himself to be swayed by sentiment or wishful thinking. Some people fall in love with a horse and expect it to perform beyond its capabilities, but not so with Val. He communicates a feeling of supreme confidence to the horse.

"Still another factor in his success is that he never sacrifices efficiency and faultless performance for speed. He avoids asking a horse to over-exert itself, but when speed is required, he seems to be able to pull it out of a horse, and it's these qualities that have made him an institution where training is concerned."

I asked Woolley questions about incidents that stand out in his mind from when Ebony Night was setting the horse show world on fire. "Yes, there were several moments, but one is etched in my memory." He paused and then went on, "It was back in '45 or '46 at the National Horse Show in Santa Barbara. All the cowboys and professional riders were out to defeat the black horse and Valdez. This particular incident was in the working cow horse class. Valdez entered the ring on Ebony Night and stationed himself in the center. The horse stood in perfect position without a move by reason of Valdez's perfect control and training. Up in the far part of the ring a big steer with large Texas-like horns entered with a ferocious attitude and appearance. He began to trot down to the center of the ring.

"At the perfect psychological moment, Val moved Ebony to cut him off and, at each and every move the steer made to get by, Valdez, with his control of the horse, would stop him. The steer was unable to get by because of the fence and the blocking performance of Ebony Night. Finally, the steer became so enraged that he turned and attempted to gore Ebony. In a split second, Val swung Ebony completely around and threw him against the side of the steer. He spun him again, striking the steer on the other side. The steer let out a raucous bellow, turned, and ran the other way. The crowd in the over-packed pavilion not only stood up and cheered but climbed on the chairs and tables, giving a true standing ovation for the performance of this great combination, Valdez and Ebony Night."

There was silence as Mr. Woolley finished his story. We both just sat for a moment; then I said, "Yes, I do remember that day; I was one of those standing and applauding the 'Dynamic Duo'."

We chatted some more and looked at the vast collection of trophies and ribbons. A feeling of emptiness crept over me as I thought about the last time I had seen the great horse. It was in 1949 that a stable fire snuffed out the life of Ebony Night.

Jimmy A. Williams: Another Legend

While I was at the River Bottom the other day looking at some horses, I stopped by the local feed store to visit. I couldn't help overhearing an old guy talking to the owner about having been around these parts years ago. He was reminiscing about all the great horsemen who rode in these arenas. He rattled off all the names of repute: M. R. Valdez, Carl Helm, Hutch Hutchison, Clyde Kennedy, and Jimmy Williams. "Jimmy was one of the greatest horsemen ever," he said.

Of course my ears pricked up, so I moved a little closer. "Some great stars, too," he added. "Robert Taylor, Clark Gable, Joel Mc-Crea, Bob Steel, Ken Maynard, Ben Johnson—those guys all rode around here a lot." He continued, "'Course, that was before your time, son . . . place has changed quite a bit since then. If those trails could talk . . . got me a book full of pictures from those old days."

I couldn't help but interrupt his rambling so I could introduce myself. "Oh yeah," he said. "You were just a wild kid back then. I remember you hanging around." We went outside and leaned on the fence. "I'm not from around here," he said. "Just used to come by a lot on my sales route." He asked mostly about the legendary Jimmy A. Williams, a topic I do know quite a bit about.

Jimmy was, quite literally, a born horseman. His father was a horse dealer and racehorse owner. His mother's family owned Standardbreds. So, he always had a horse to ride while growing up—Saddlebreds, hunters, cow ponies—anything with four legs, a mane, and a tail.

In 1932, as a teenager, he was hired by the Los Angeles Sale Barn to ride and show the animals to prospective buyers. On Sundays, he rode in the "Lap and Tap" Quarter Horse races at Huntington Beach and raced Thoroughbreds on the California fair circuit. For years, Coca-Cola ads featured a photo of Jimmy taken during one of these races.

It was while riding at one of the sales that a "scout" from MGM approached Jimmy to try out as a double for Tyrone Power. Being not only a good rider, but also bearing a fairly good resemblance to the late actor, he was selected from thirty others for the riding scenes in the film *Marie Antoinette*. When Power, on loan to MGM, returned to 20th Century Fox, his new "double" went on the payroll at $50 a week, just to be on standby.

Even though fifty a week was a princely sum in those days, Jimmy was able to supplement that quite regularly by taking stunt jobs on other films, as long as they didn't conflict with his "on call" status. Jimmy worked on a lot of Power's pictures, including *Suez* and *Jesse James*. But he's most noted for his stunts in *The Mark of Zorro*.

Jimmy was also known as a ladies' man. The story goes that when he doubled Tyrone Power, being equally as good looking, Jimmy always left with the girl at the end of the day's work.

By now, World War II had erupted and Jimmy went into the Army. He served in Africa and Europe until he was wounded in Italy. As he recuperated, it was discovered that he was a horseman, and Tech Sergeant Williams was transferred to the 2610th Remount with a raise in rating to Master Sergeant. Using captured and "liberated" horses and mules from Italy, Africa, and the Near East, the "Brass" had him organize an animal variety show. He went on tour and entertained the troops with musical chairs, races, bucking horses, and mules.

In addition to the horse and mule variety show, an informal team was put together consisting of Sergeant Williams, Lieutenant

Kurtz, and Major Burkholder. In 1945, with their motley assortment of livestock, they were able to beat the Italian and British teams in competition over fences in Florence, Italy.

It was during this period that Jimmy learned about dressage training, discovering how it can be applied to any type of horse. After the war, Jimmy began training horses and incorporated the European dressage techniques he had learned. Western horses, jumpers, racehorses, polo ponies—all responded perfectly to this "new" way of training. He credited this, more than anything else, for the great strides his horsemanship career took after that time.

Another of Jimmy's success formulas was that all of his training had a Western slant. Because of his many championships, he made "stock horse" a household word before stock horse competition evolved into reining. Even his jumpers could turn on their hindquarters and generally perform like a stock horse (or reining horse). And he didn't quit there; he even had his dog trained to perform that way. I'm sure if he were with us today they would be holding cutting pup futurities!

He was a gadgeteer and an innovator, always dreaming up something that he thought might solve a problem with an unruly horse. In fact, he laughed at me for always having my head in his horse's mouth to see if there was some new invention.

Which brings me to the story of how he used to drive all of his horses to a cart. It was not just an ordinary cart, but one equipped with brakes, levers, pulleys, and all types of other gadgets. Jimmy would arrive at the show with forty or more horses and, naturally, was the center of attention. He created quite an interest among the other professionals because all of his winning horses were being driven to this cart. He delighted in telling people about the special brake system that he could control to teach a horse to change leads, or the special wiring for electricity to get one to back up or stop, and all the special harness that could make a horse a champion in thirty days.

Needless to say, I (along with all the rest) couldn't resist the temptation. I bought a cart and rigged it just like his. I had just acquired a horse that had been at Jimmy's barn for over a year. So, I thought to myself, I'll hitch this horse up and learn how he responds to all the gadgets, and I too will win everything. (I found out later there were more carts sold at that time than ever before.)

I rigged this horse up to the cart and he stood there like a trooper. When I gave him the signal to move out, he did so, with dispatch. We walked around the ring and turned right and left. I was busting my buttons as I used the brakes and pulleys and ropes I had hung all over him. Needing more room to maneuver, we went out to the big jumping field where I could extend his gaits. After trotting awhile, I asked him to canter so I could cue him to change leads and see how the brakes helped in teaching this. I urged him forward into the canter . . . faster and faster we went.

Thinking I'd better change direction before he picked up more speed, I did so and applied the brake at the same time. The cart started to slide sideways because, as I was later told, you applied the one brake in the direction you wanted to go, which locks that wheel. The wheel locked all right, and we almost spun out as the horse gained momentum.

I used another "aid" which only stampeded the horse further. Racing out of control, I could see us heading right toward a red and white post-and-rail jump standing about 4'6" high. Yes, the horse jumped, but neither the cart nor I made it. After the final impact, I surveyed the damage. Everything was upside down—a wheel here, part of a harness there, the horse running loose—and myself all skinned up.

I picked up the pieces and went right to the phone and called Jimmy. "Oh, Don," he said, "that's the only horse I've never driven—and frankly, I only did all that driving business for show and conversation. You, of all people, should know that." A lesson I've never forgotten.

Ever a showman, Jimmy liked to peel off the bridle, fold his arms, cut a cow, jump a fence, or spin around, always with that subtle grin and the phrase "My horses love me!"

I think the best-remembered thing about Jimmy was his sayings. He had one for every occasion. My favorite that his father used to preach was emblazoned on Jimmy's golf cart: "It's what you learn after you know it all that counts." I feel fortunate to have been given one of the few copies of his book of sayings and will share the following two: "Sometimes you have to be silent to be heard," and "A horse is like a house, no better than its foundation."

Clyde Kennedy: Numero Uno

The Los Angeles Police Chief invariably referred to him as "Numero Uno," because he had created the mounted police patrol for the city. Being a legendary horseman, whipping into shape the untrained horses and riders (for crowd control and street patrol) became a challenge that obviously utilized his many talents. He even had a special badge that he often flashed to get into places where tickets were required. "C'mon," he'd say, "let's get in for free."

That was his last training job. Clyde Kennedy passed away in May, 1995.

Clyde's sister, Betty, called just recently to tell me that Tucson Bar had died. The big, striking gray not only was a champion show horse but also could do more tricks than Harry Houdini. Clyde always had with him a favorite horse of the time and I believe Tucson Bar was his all-time favorite and friend.

Clyde also always had a trained dog. "Junior" was the dog I remember when I was around, an Australian Shepherd who could match any of Clyde's horses, trick for trick.

Clyde was a born prankster, which encouraged a passel of stories to circulate. Everyone that came in contact with him had a Clyde Kennedy story. I have many, as I probably had known him longer than anyone (other than relatives).

As a kid, I grew up riding in the River Bottom and tagging along with Clyde. Growing into my teens, I galloped racehorses for Clyde's father, George, and upon my discharge from the Navy in 1950, I went to work with Clyde. We shared the same house for several years before I hung up my own shingle.

In fact, he inadvertently started my literary career. The first story I ever wrote was about Clyde winning the stock horse class (now called reining) at the Chicago International. He rode to a standing ovation on a horse called Rango. I received an "F" for spelling and punctuation, but an "A" for content. I started with a capital and five hundred words later ended with a period. I learned to punctuate after that.

During the decade of the 50s, the horse business was booming. Everybody showed every kind of horse (breed and discipline) in order to make a living. Hardly anyone was a specialist in those days, which fostered a sense of camaraderie. We'd compete as hard as we could against each other during the day, and then gather for eats and drinks at night. If you won the "Stake" class, it was your turn to host a barn party, which probably cost you more than you had won.

In my opinion, Clyde epitomizes the man of many hats, or the best seat-of-the-pants rider that ever came along. He had done just about everything there was to do with a horse, from jumping over cars to being voted Horseman of the Year in 1963. In the beginning, to augment his income, he doubled as a stuntman for many stars—riding over cliffs or jumping through burning storefronts. If you saw an Indian carrying a flaming torch over a barricade of wagons, it was probably Clyde. In his Hollywood daredevil days, special effects were scarce—if it was on fire, it was really burning. Being of medium build, Clyde was able to double both men and women, and in later years enjoyed fooling the judge by showing up in a ladies class in makeup, wig, and costume.

He doubled for Elizabeth Taylor in *National Velvet* and several times for Abbott and Costello. Once while stunting for Costello, Clyde was to swing down from a barn loft on a pulley attached to a cable several hundred feet in front of the barn and land on the back of a surprised horse . . . backwards yet! Then a hidden handler turned the horse loose and the script called for Clyde to ride over the rails of the racetrack, still riding backwards. It was filmed successfully on the first take; Clyde was that good.

Clyde had a lot of movie personalities as clients and we even had song-and-dance man Dan Dailey for a neighbor. One day there were several actors at the barn: Dan, Tab Hunter, Guy Mitchell, and Slim Pickens. Slim had with him a chicken. Why? I have no idea, but somehow the chicken got loose. As Clyde was walking through the barn to answer the phone, he saw a brand new customer drive in and run over the chicken. While everyone else was out back in the arena, Clyde convinced the visitor that he had just killed the only trained falling chicken in the world. The story went on that Slim had stopped by to school the chicken for a picture job starting that afternoon. Several thousands of dollars were at stake, Clyde told him, and he must face up to Slim and compensate him for the loss of both chicken and revenue. We all fell in with the charade and it wasn't until the customer was actually writing the check that the truth came out.

Being somewhat of a clown at times, Clyde usually did the unexpected. He had another favorite horse, The Mad Frenchman, that he'd jump over the in-gate into the arena, jump the course, and then jump over the out-gate. Then, more often than not, he'd quickly change saddles and jump Frenchy into the other ring to show in the cutting.

Clyde showed a lot of polo ponies too, and during one such class, I remember, he went off course. Colonel Alex Sysin was the ringmaster, dressed in a tuxedo and carrying a cane that he would wave around with each command. After Colonel Sysin waved him out and was leaning on his cane, Clyde, on his way out of the arena, made a detour and with a backhand shot knocked the cane out from under Alex. Everyone held their breath, as we watched him teeter back and forth, but he never fell.

As a tagalong kid, I remember well that Clyde would always be the last to leave the table at a restaurant. He'd gather up all the tips left by everyone else and then find the waitress so she'd think he was the big tipper in the crowd.

During the years I hauled with Clyde, I'm not sure I ever saw the last class of the show. When he finished showing, he'd be out the gate and into the van, unsaddling along the way, then load up and head out. He used to tell me (as did my dad and granddad) that the saddest sight is an empty showgrounds after the show is over.

He could be devilish one minute and the greatest help the next, without needing to be asked. A couple of times come to memory. Once, at the State Fair in Sacramento, Ora Rhodes, a popular trainer at that time, had two horses entered in the Stock Horse Stake. Just minutes before the class, a heart attack forced him to the emergency room in an ambulance. Clyde mounted one of Ora's horses and Jimmy Williams got on the other, catch riding to first and second; beating even their own trained mounts.

Another time when Red Neil fell ill, without the slightest hesitation Clyde drove a hundred miles each way for many days to make sure Red's horses were worked, before ever working his own.

As great as his success was as a trainer, he easily moved into the arena as a judge, holding cards in most AHSA divisions. He judged the very first AQHA World Show and many other shows in foreign countries. His globetrotting added more stories to the many judge's rooms, one being his deep affection for young people. He never tired of giving advice from a judge's viewpoint, and his students reaped his wisdom and unique understanding of the nature of horse and rider working together as a team.

Another story that I'll relate happened while he was judging in Italy. He decided to hold a clinic and assembled all the youth at the end of the show. After lecturing for a long time, singling out each one, someone finally told him that not one of the students understood English. This didn't deter Clyde—he simply got on a horse and *showed* them how to do it.

Today, his former students—especially those fortunate enough to have ridden another favorite horse, Julio—still regard Clyde as the best horsemanship teacher of the era.

Clyde was the consummate trainer. He ate and slept training horses, and anything that moved. I know for a fact he trained horses in his sleep because he would wake me up in the middle of the night yelling "Whoa, whoa," or "Come on pardner, only one jump left." Even when it was supposed to be time off, he'd load up a horse and go somewhere to ride. In my mind, there will always be one more jump for this legendary horse world great.

Andy Jauregui:
A Cowboy's Cowboy

There are many great horsemen (present and past) who have never shown a horse at a horse show. In my quest to increase awareness of these people, special to the industry, one such legend comes to mind—Andy Jauregui.

I remember the time I went to visit him in retirement. His ranch house could have been the scene for a thousand Western movies, complete with Navajo rugs, pictures of great men and horses, and trophies and awards too numerous to describe. Camille (Andy's wife of forever) was busy in the kitchen as we began to relive the life of the man just inducted into the Cowboy Hall of Fame.

Now I'd known Andy for years, not only as a cowboy and rodeo stock contractor, but more as a true horseman or reinsman who had the feel it took to make great horses. Though Andy was born on a sheep ranch in Ventura County, California, sheep soon gave way to horses as the Yanez Ranch, next door, turned out some of the best working horses around. During his childhood he learned the meaning of "good hands," which was to become his trademark in later years.

His rodeo career started when a producer named Jesse Stahl (who, by coincidence, was inducted into the Cowboy Hall of Fame at the same time Andy was) came through town, putting on his shows. Andy was fifteen at the time and rode bucking horses for $2.00 a ride. After riding broncs a while, his interest soon turned to roping where he would become the World Champion Steer Roper in 1931 and the World Champion Team Roper in 1934.

We reviewed his varied and colorful career as we talked . . . occasions such as when he rode horseback from Ventura to the far San Bernardino Mountains. "Ride one and lead one," he said. "Nothing but a bedroll." Or how he and Camille spent their honeymoon living in a tent by a stream, wrangling dude horses. He even spent some years as a Hollywood stuntman, doubling some of the stars of yesterday. He did the falls, the chases, and the daring challenges that were all part of the job. There were the all-night drives to the rodeos, the missed loops, and the adulation that comes from winning . . . if it was to be done, Andy did it.

But being the true family man that he was, he began to stay closer to home after his children arrived. Not far from where we were now sitting, in a town called Newhall, California, he and a movie stock contractor named "Fat" Jones went into a partnership on some cattle and, later, on some horses.

This eventually led Andy to form his famous Jay Spear Rodeo Company. The Jay Spear would become known for its quality stock horses, hard-to-ride bulls, and stout-roping cattle. He produced rodeos everywhere and furnished stock for the first rodeo finals ever held. Cowboys from near and far followed this man with the magic grin.

Throughout all of his career, the lean years and the heights, he always rode a top horse, which he personally picked out and trained. People in all parts of the horse business sought his expertise and knowledge. His rope horses were schooled to perfection and were envied by those he competed against. He mounted many famous cowboys so they could "go for the money." Men like Ben Johnson, who went on to become a star in another field, had the opportunity to ride a Jauregui horse.

Growing up, I knew of the famous Andy, but my personal experience came through show horses and not rodeo. I happened upon the Jauregui Ranch many years ago when Clyde Kennedy and I had gone to look at a bridle horse. We drove down the same driveway by pastures filled with horses and cattle and a big tree, which, I was to learn, was his "training tree." Several horses, bitted up and fastened to the limbs above, stood around the base.

We talked and listened to Andy's training methods. "Time and a little bit of work (often) . . . don't overdo . . . you can't teach a tired horse anything," he said. "I ride 'em awhile, follow some cattle, gather some horses, put 'em on the training tree, ride 'em a little more . . . keep 'em happy is my motto." We made our way to the famous tree to take a closer look at a horse Clyde had had his eye on when we drove in. True form to function, that horse could do everything and never put a foot out of place! Yes, we loaded the horse and took him home and he soon became the champion his basics allowed him to be.

"You know, Don," Andy said, "at one time I schooled a lot of polo ponies. They had to be shifty and fast, but most of all, they had to handle." I then remembered the friendship he had had with Will Rogers, as Will always did like a good horse and Andy sold or traded him many. We talked of others who, through the appreciation of good horses, had become best friends with Andy. One of my favorites was actor Joel McCrea, who looked more at home on a horse than anywhere else. Andy told me of their close relationship. "Now there's a fella who's a real cowboy. He knew a good horse and only used those kind in his pictures." It was the highest compliment that Andy could give to anyone.

The day was coming to a close. Andy walked me to the door and I stood on the porch for a moment looking out at the tree— his training tree—and I imagined I saw horses standing around it once again. It seemed like the pastures were filled with cattle, the arena alive with activity; ghosts, perhaps. I don't know, but as I drove out I looked in my rearview mirror and saw the man standing alone on the porch, silhouetted in the setting sun, and I thought to myself, "There is truly a cowboy's cowboy."

Mac McHugh:
Cowboy Artist

I was never around for any of my high school reunions but when I received an invitation to participate in a horse show roundup of old-timers, I just had to go. It was an evening dedicated to the remembrance of the horses, riders, owners, trainers, and officials of shows during the fifties. There were more horses ridden, stories told, and people talked about in one night than in that whole decade. A large display of vintage pictures filled one wall and at each place setting was a reminder list of those who had passed on.

The next morning I got out some old horse magazines and came across an article titled, "Mac McHugh, Cowboy Artist." He had been a longtime friend and on last night's "list." Turning back the clock, I remembered when he opened his first training stable in the Mission Valley area of San Diego, California. In those days we referred to him as the "Chinese Cowboy," a moniker derived from his Hong Kong birthplace, regardless of his parents' American heritage.

He called himself Frank, but, as nicknames have a way of clinging like barnacles, it was always "hey Mac, you're next to go," or "hey Mac, where's my rope?" It wasn't long until he became Mac McHugh, even to himself. He was a horseman, superb trainer, and artist par excellence. He said to me once, "I'm the luckiest person in the world; I work with the people I like and the horses I love." I remember some of the people: the ropers he started riding with when he acquired the bug; the group he rode with on Rancheros (the famous 4Q's camp); other horsemen, like Jimmy Williams, for whom he designed bits and equipment; and Billy Harris, whom he counseled.

Many champion horses that were never sold lived the good life at Mac's Bien Tiempo Ranch well into their twenties. There was Hooker D, a great little cow horse whose heart far exceeded his size. He was rewarded with championships too numerous to list and, because of his great record, was inducted into the Cow Horse Hall of Fame in 1977. Then there was Seatac, a champion pleasure horse, and the year after year hackamore champions from the Gibson Ranch (which Mac rode for in the 50s and 60s). Mac not only had Western horses but, after his marriage to jumping horse rider Margaret Sullivan (whom I remember as a young girl rode a horse called Fiddlesticks that had a very unique jumping style), he also owned a champion jumper named Notice Me . . . and everyone did!

I remembered the trail horses he schooled that set the trend for today's competitions, and the leadership he gave to the horse organizations he belonged to. He was outspoken when he thought he was right—to some even a little bullheaded at times—but all leaders are like that, I guess. He was always called upon to design a multitude of things for organizations, such as logos. Even my business logo was a McHugh original.

Not only was he one of the finest artists to graduate from Otis Art Institute, but his art took on many forms. Some of Mac's original paintings grace the homes of movie stars Roy Rogers and Rocky Lane. What I remember most are his pencil sketches and drawings. These included horses like Honeymoon, and horses and riders such as George Wolfe upon Whirlaway, Johnny Longden on With Regards, Ray York on Kentucky Derby winner Determine, the famous roping horse Devil Dust, and a head of Man O'War, done for singer Dennis Day.

Another of Mac's artistic accomplishments were his "Burn-Tone Originals," created by a special wood-burning technique. He did one panel that measured eight feet in length and was four feet high. It had thirty figures including men, horses, and cattle that depicted the pedigree of the famous Quarter Horse stallion Joe Barrett. The panel was displayed to much acclaim at the 1949 Denver Livestock Show and has since been reproduced in several magazines.

His art talent surfaced numerous times on the covers of *The Thoroughbred Magazine* when it first started out, and *The Quarter Horse Journal* in its infancy. His illustrations also grace the Quarter Horse Stud Books.

Mac used his artistic way of looking at things to further his horse training techniques, which, in 1981, led to his being named California Professional Horsemen's Association "Horseman of the Year." In 1982, his wife and partner in the training business was honored as "Horsewoman of the Year."

Mac had a unique sense of humor, which not only showed up in his cartoons but in the skits he wrote and directed for numerous horsemen's social events throughout the years.

I used to kid Mac about how much he could abuse his gastronomical habits and still stay so lean. I remember his ever-ready answer: he had only 20 percent of his stomach remaining (the result of a wartime injury he sustained while serving aboard the USS *Lexington*).

Mac and I hauled horses a lot together in the 50s and, as the story goes, we were neck and neck for the year-end championship. We were both standing outside the ring waiting to show in a halter class. We were so deep in conversation that neither of us noticed the practical joker who switched our lead shanks. The gate opened and I nonchalantly led his horse and he led mine. Once inside, we couldn't change horses. Naturally I won but lost in the end, as his horse beat mine.

Now that the AQHA headquarters has undergone a facelift, you will discover many drawings and paintings while walking the corridors. Several of these are by Mac McHugh.

Rex Peterson: Trick Horse Trainer

In my travels, I've had the opportunity to visit with great horse-men all over the world, which is one of the rewards of being in this business. I first became aware of Rex Peterson several years ago when he was winning in the show ring. As it happens often where the Quarter Horse is the main ingredient, our paths crossed again, this time at the sneak preview of Black Beauty. I was waiting to meet the producer, director, and trainer when a familiar face peeked out from behind a finely preened handlebar moustache.

Yes, from show horse trainer to trick horse expert and winner of special awards—AQHA's Silver Spur award for *Black Beauty* and previously the "Patsy" for the film *Sylvester*—a horseman and his horses were indeed being recognized. After we reminisced in the lobby, our paths were destined to cross many times as the AQHA, Black Beauty, and Rex were to become allies.

We visited at his ranch during a shoot for *America's Horse* and again in Fort Worth at the Junior World Show, where we made a date to kick back and discuss the tricks of the trade upon our re-turn home. During these occasions, perfection was witnessed as Rex schooled Justin (Docs Keepin Time) for his many perform-ances as Black Beauty. I was so impressed with the bond that was exhibited between horse and horseman; it became evident that there wasn't much of anything that this horse wouldn't do for him.

The day of the interview, I arrived early and was greeted by both sons, Tyler and Ryan (ages 4 and 3), turned out in hat, chaps, boots, and spurs, ready to play cowboy. Brenda, Rex's wife, had steaming black coffee waiting and we delved into the great horses of the past whose careers left an indelible mark in the memory of moviegoers everywhere.

Horses named Steel, Dice, Reno, and Prince, who carried all the great Western actors and actresses and would be recognized on the screen but not by name. The trainers who, behind the scenes, made the movie legends: Ralph McCutcheon, Les Hilton, Dyke Johnson, and of course the master himself, Glenn Randall.

Our conversation got around to how and why he switched from show horses to movie horses. "Don," he said, "for a kid from Nebraska who grew up around the Haythorn Ranch ridin' and ropin', when Glenn Randall came to town with the *Ben Hur* chariot horse act, I knew I had found my calling. I never dreamed horses could do things like that. I tried trick riding, Roman riding with my brothers, and even had a liberty act with my sister and brothers.

"As soon as I was old enough, I shipped to California and signed on with Glenn. I had to show reiners, jumpers, and dressage horses along the way while learning what makes a horse tick. At the Randall Ranch, I was considered a rider but I had other ideas. I'd watch Glenn with eagle eyes and after work I'd try what he did on my own horse, Casey. I'd usually get in trouble and Glenn would have to bail me out, but after a few years I kinda got the hang of it; even made Glenn a little proud too, as he watched Casey perform more and more tricks."

Rex got pretty serious as he talked about Casey. Casey was his first school horse, a three-year-old when Rex started training him. Having taught him everything to perfection, Rex became quite dejected when he lost the horse. "I sort of quit the trick business for awhile and just showed. I felt I lost part of me," he said.

I recognized the common thread evident among all great horsemen. They actually live, breathe, and talk horses seven days a week, twenty-four hours a day. Horse psychology comes from everyday work. Think like the horse, develop trust, and concentrate 110 percent. Timing is everything, knowing when to quit or back off or go forward. Rex learned to control his temper, which is the first prerequisite to training any horse. Glenn embodied the principle of being satisfied with just one step at a time, not hurrying or tiring a horse out, and giving short lessons, often.

I asked Rex about the whips he uses. "They're just tools of the trade, an extension of the arm. The whip simply guides. The horse can see more and from farther away when I use them. I have to have instant control and recognition to keep the horse focused on me when hundreds of people and cameras are moving about. However, any tool must be used correctly, because a horse can't work out of fear."

A firm believer in the knowledge of basic dressage, Rex touts and uses this discipline in all his training procedures. He was smart enough to understand this early on and quickly stresses its importance in the training of any horse.

We swapped horse stories and he divulged a few training secrets he told me not to print. He then went on about the job he did with Justin for a music video. Seems the script called for Rex to bury Justin completely and on cue, he was to burst out of the ground. Can you imagine a horse being totally buried, head to tail, and waiting until the director says, "Action," before rising as if from the dead? This was one secret I couldn't pry out of him.

It's comman knowledge that because of disposition and athletic ability, the Quarter Horse has been the popular choice of stars and movie trainers for years. Rex is doing his best to make that fact even more well known. If you saw the movie *Black Beauty*, I'm sure you noticed Justin was listed first in the credits as "Docs Keepin Time, an American Quarter Horse."

As I got ready to leave, Rex said he needed to stop by the barn and put away his tack. "Went ropin' last night and got in a little late," he confided. Because of his background, I asked him if he still threw a side-arm loop. He just laughed. "Yeah," he said. "Some things never change."

PART IV

PERSONAL MEMORIES

A Trunk Full of Memories

Ah, nostalgia. What a wonderful thing. Maybe I was thinking of AQHA's historical marker program (I've been fortunate to dedicate a few) that turns a chosen site, great horses, and people of the past into a memory that lives on. Or maybe it was my two riding granddaughters who prompted me to open my old tack trunk that had been tucked away in my office under an old Navajo blanket. I'd forgotten what it contained. Probably bits and spurs made long before I was even born, that were used daily by my granddaddy, my dad, and even me when I was a young ridin' fool.

I lifted the lid, revealing relics of my past to two eager faces that insisted on a story about each object. A couple of ropes and a reata brought back memories of snubbin' posts and breakin' colts.

When we broke colts, my granddaddy would sack 'em out (not a lot of finesse back then), saddle 'em, and holler for me. Then he'd get on a big stout horse we called Stub and my dad would maneuver around and put me on the colt. My granddaddy would take a dally with what he called a come-here-rope (kinda like a war bridle) and pony me around the bullpen. When he thought it was okay, we'd graduate to a larger corral where he'd fish me enough line until we were kinda ridin' side by side. This worked great except once when the line got a little lax (maybe ten to twelve feet between us), the big old colt I was on broke in two. He didn't buck me off but succeeded in jumping over the fence. I was trying to stay on and my granddaddy was trying to snub the colt from the other side of the fence. When the near disaster was over, he looked at me and said, "What in the H . . . did you let him do that for?" My granddaddy was a no-nonsense kind of a guy.

Uncovering a rusty old .22 rifle I carried when I was a kid reminded me of the first time I killed a rattler. I was ambling along and decided to take a shortcut home (five miles away). Down the mountainside I went and came smack dab up against about a three-foot rattlesnake. I steadied my horse and shot the snake. I was taught that after you killed a rattlesnake, you cut off the head and rattles. Well, I cut off the rattles all right but when I started to cut off his head, I must have cut a nerve because that snake wrapped himself around my arm so fast, I thought I was a goner. I threw up my hands, lost my horse, and tumbled down about thirty feet of hillside trying to get it off my arm. By the time I had shaken the snake loose, my pony had gone on home and I was left afoot in boots that weren't made for walkin'.

We waded through old pieces of leather (I wondered why I had kept them), and a scrapbook full of pictures from long ago when I used to jump over cars on horseback for a few dollars. They were interested in the one where my horse slipped on take-off and scrambled through the air. It looked like I was trying to dismount from the expression on my face, the horse's, as well as the face of the guy who owned the car. But I had assured him the secret to riding jumping horses was to be *on* the horse when it landed. Ah, youth . . . I was the eternal optimist.

We dug out an old stirrup that was mashed flat, which reminded me why my foot hurts every now and then. So I retold the story of how I ended up in a body cast for about a year. It was great to have a captive audience who wanted to know every detail.

Rummaging around, we found my old chaps, which each girl wanted to try on, and an old hunt coat that still had my number pinned on the back from the last jumping class I had entered, many moons ago. At that time, I hadn't shown in a jumping class for a while but some former clients had bought a horse and needed me to show him. He was a tough one. He'd jump a couple of fences and then would try to buck you off somewhere on the course when you'd least expect it. I flew in, rode the horse, won the championship, and flew out. I'll always remember that ride because the horse bucked more and more as the ride went on, but I guess he was just making sure he'd give me something to look back on.

It was time to close the trunk, as supper was ready. I went to sleep that night with a smile on my face and visions of horse stories prancing in my head.

Now there are a couple of things that happen when you get older; the stories probably get embellished and it's harder to get through the night without going to the bathroom. As we would be flying East the next day, the alarm was set very early. I usually don't turn on the light (abiding by my wife's desires) but instead grope, bump into things, groan, and wake her up anyway. For some unknown reason, this night I tried to turn on the light. Nothing. "What are you doing?" she moaned, as I fumbled for another switch. No power! I panicked. I couldn't even read my watch. She finally found a flashlight and I looked at the time. We were late. Horrors! We found the ever-ready candles and moved our bodies into "fast forward." With no heat, no electric razor, a cold shower, and only candlelight to pack by, we scrambled to the airport and boarded our plane just as the door closed.

My romantic vision of the day before had rapidly changed to the reality of today. However, once I settled in my seat, I closed my eyes, pushed rewind in my mind, and up popped nostalgia once again. It was a nice flight.

Chief Rojas:
Legendary Ground Man

J ust about a moon ago, I was a clinician at the Virginia Horse
Festival in Lexington. Afterwards, Ardy and I decided to stay a
couple of days and roam the historic countryside. As we drove the
back roads, we found out-of-the-way, cozy inns for our lodging.
One such place was in Woodstock where we actually slept in the
bedroom once used by Stonewall Jackson when he headquartered
there during his battles in the Shenandoah Valley.

Our trek also took us into the hunt country of Upperville and
Middleburg. We visited steeplechase farms and facilities specializing
in field hunters and hounds. Some of the top hunter, jumper, and
eventing trainers reside in that area, along with a few cowboys.

In talking with the top professionals from all fields, it became
quite evident that one secret to their success was having a good
ground man (or woman). Most were experienced, had been around a
long time, and didn't ride much but had a good eye for what the
horse and trainer were doing, good and bad. Their counsel and ability
to read the situation was the paramount reason for success.

After visiting with them, I reflected on one such ground man who
was a legend in California history during the 1950s and 60s. He was
sort of a gypsy and claimed to be part Indian and part Spaniard; but
mostly horse. He called himself "Chief," even though his real name
was Arnold Rojas. He would just show up at my place and those of
other trainers up and down the state. I'd head for the barn early in
the morning and there would be the familiar pickup hosting a
camper box with Chief sitting in the doorway waiting for me. No notice or call, he'd just be there. He floated teeth, watched me school

horses, advised me from his standpoint, and just as mysteriously as he appeared, one morning he'd be gone. No goodbyes or see-you-laters—he'd just disappear like an Indian in the night.

No one really knew how old he was because for the nearly twenty years he was around my place, he always looked the same. I never saw him ride, but every so often he would catch one of my horses, groom him to perfection, put on his saddle and silver bridle, tie a hair rope with an elaborate knot around the horse's neck, and put a neatly coiled reata (each coil of exactly the same dimension) on the saddle. But he'd never get on. Instead, he'd take the slack out of the reins, wrap them around the horn, and turn him into a pen. The horse always did the same thing. He'd arch his neck, prick his ears forward, and, with his tongue, twirl the cricket in the spade bit to create the noise that always brought a smile to Chief's face. "Ah, musica," he would say.

As I was young and an eager student, sometimes he would smooth a place on the ground and with a sharp stick draw many different types of mouthpieces. I recall the first time he drew out the different styles of "Chileno" (Mexican ring bits). Each one had a different quality from the other. The mouthpiece of the Andalusian bit sloped from the cheeks to the center where it arched to bridge the tongue so as not to pinch. What he called the "mustache of the moor" had a curved bar and low port. "Very mild," he would say. "Los Barrels" had oblong barrels of copper around the steel that he termed "los sabores" (the flavors), to sweeten the mouth.

There were several things I remember he told me never to do. Never try to teach a colt something new until he has mastered all of what he has already been taught. Never lose sight of a horse's ears because by their movement he indicates his intentions. Never put your saddle on a horse that bears the brand of the goat. This brand is easily seen on the knees of a horse that has fallen many times. He is marked for life and unsafe to ride.

It is not true, he told me, that the longer the horse is ridden in a hackamore and without the bit, the better rein he will have. The horse should have a bit put in his mouth when he asks for it. His favorite saying, at least to me, was "The devil is not such a devil because he is the devil; but because of the years he spent practicing." In relationship, good horses and good horsemen are like "him" in this respect. In fact, almost all winners follow Chief's philosophy: they listen and take direction from whatever the title, coach, ground man, advisor, or analyst.

Our final stop was in John Mosby territory, where we stayed the night at a tavern and inn that the infamous raider had frequented and thus was named after. It was like a museum of hunting history. We were given a choice of two rooms, which the innkeeper indicated on the brochure she handed us. She pointed to the stairs and said the doors were open. We quickly decided on number 21, as it had a canopy bed and a private bath.

Ardy got the key, I toted the luggage, working up a puff or two, and we settled into the Martha Washington room. Deciding we had time to do more sightseeing before dinner, we tried to lock our room but to no avail. Ardy decided the innkeeper had given us the wrong key and went downstairs. Climbing two steps at a time, she said, breathlessly, "Honey! We don't have the wrong key, we're in the wrong room and the other couple is downstairs now. We belong next door."

As we scrambled to switch rooms, my wife made sure we didn't leave any telltale evidence behind and left the door ajar. Ardy couldn't believe she had made a mistake and rechecked the brochure. Yup, she had misread the room numbers. We were supposed to be in room 20, the Bridal Suite (of all places), which turned out to be much nicer than Martha's room. Seems we should have followed what we just had been discussing and paid more attention to those giving direction.

Ray York: Gutsy Jockey

I know I'm dating myself but one night while I had my boots off and feet up in front of a glowing fire, I reflected on an old Perry Como song, "Find a wheel and it goes round, round, round." It brought to mind that staying in touch with old friends is a must.

I talked the other evening with just such an old friend who began the conversation with, "You wanna hear the latest news?" Before I could answer, Jay Fishburn, who was the leading Quarter Horse jockey of 1959, went into a long spiel on the day's events. Seems he, being a retired jockey as well as a second unit director on too many movies to list, had attended a jockey's get-together luncheon at a cafe in Del Mar, California. Jay rattled off the names so fast it was hard to take notes. Legends like Johnny Longden in his nineties, Bill Shoemaker still active even after his paralyzing accident, Don Pierce, Alex Maze, Bill Harmatz, and Ray York, a name from my past.

"Do you know what Ray's going to do?" He blurted out. "He's gonna ride a race—a real race—not one of those rocking chair derbies." I was surprised, but not very, because the Ray York I knew and palled around with in the 50s was always a gutsy guy.

As the story goes, Ray had announced at the get-together that he was going to set a record by becoming the first jockey ever to ride real pari-mutuel races in seven different decades. Having just turned sixty-six, he still weighed in at 113 pounds. One former jockey commented, "He may be sixty-six years old but he has the body of a man forty-five and the mind of a twenty-one-year-old."

Ray started riding match races in San Diego in the late 40s, won the Kentucky Derby with Determine in 1954, was awarded the George Wolfe Memorial Trophy for outstanding contribution, and as one of the country's leading jockeys, has netted 3,082 winning races. In his retirement years, Ray also worked in the picture business. But until Thursday, January 13th, 2000, he hadn't ridden in a pari-mutuel race since 1992. His mount was a horse named Culebra, owned by a friend of all of ours from way back, legendary trainer Henry Moreno.

Henry hails from the famous Moreno clan, who were heavy Quarter Horse supporters in that same era. In fact, Henry trained horses and was best friends with Dr. Billy Linfoot, whom I refer to quite often as an original horse whisperer. If you review the race winners of bygone days, the name of the sire of many winners shows up on the papers as Little Request, a horse owned by Henry and reportedly to have sold for $100,000, which was unheard of in those days.

But back to Ray. He not only rode racers but also cutting and jumping horses—"anything with hair," he would say. A compadre of Slim Pickens and Clyde Kennedy, he spent as much time at shows as he did at the track. I called him after I heard the news and we set up a rendezvous to meet at Clocker's Corner at Santa Anita, 8:00 A.M., Wednesday. It would be Ray, Henry, Jay, his wife Donna Hall Fishburn, and me.

Breakfast then turned into a full-blown, four-hour-plus reunion, reliving our younger days. At the table, Ray was deluged with owners, trainers, and other jockeys who stopped by to say hello. He once again is getting phone calls from all over the world for interviews and appearances on TV. He said it took him two hours just to get out of the jock's room after the race.

We recalled the 50s when we hung out at his restaurant called the Skate and Spur and then took turns relating all the horsemen we had known. He and Henry Moreno had been fast friends since the 40s. As an aside, the man who first taught the art of horse whispering, Frank Moon, an Indian drifter from Canada, made his headquarters at the Moreno ranch. Henry and his famous relatives had every kind of horse imaginable, and today he is in partnership with leading Quarter Horse trainer, Blane Schvaneveldt, on a stallion named Red.

The little guy with the big heart became ten feet tall and was truly moved when he told of dismounting and finding Johnny Longden and champion roper and friend, Holloway Grace (both in their nineties), waiting for him. Henry made a present of the horse to Ray so he could take him home to remember the ride.

I found out he had been galloping horses at Santa Anita for the past couple of months, getting in shape. He said Henry put him on sixty-two horses in ten days and after galloping about twenty, he vaulted off, as in days of yore, only to find out he couldn't straighten up for a few minutes.

He finished tenth in the race, but said to a reporter, "I'm the happiest man in the world; I just broke a record." Culebra, a 37-1 longshot, was in contention down the backstretch but lost ground rapidly in the stretch. Ray was quoted, "I rode the horse better than the horse ran."

Even though I was in Las Vegas attending the American Horse Shows Association convention, a couple of other senior citizen friends of Ray's and I put $20 on the nose for old-time's sake. When the Friday paper came out with the story, the headline read, "Jockey York 10th, but he's still first."

I asked Ray if he planned to ride another race. He grinned as he said, "For Henry, maybe, if he could guarantee a winner." Henry gave us a little wink and said he just might come up with one. You can bet your boots I'll be there!

The Breakfast Club

There is a loose thread invisibly woven between all horse people (regardless of what they do with their horses) that is linked to their epicurean tastes. Whether in their hometown or on the road, there are always those places that they "must stop at" or "must take you to." There was one such famous place (more than an eatery) that later became the watering hole we all frequented.

Victor McLaughlin Stadium occupied the corner of Riverside Drive and Los Feliz Boulevard and housed his famous Light Horse Troop Drill Team. It later became the Horse Palace where people either shipped their horses in by railroad car from all over the nation, or rode them from nearby stables to perform nearly year-round. It was the hub of horse activity and drew notables from many circles.

The adjacent Breakfast Club originated in 1925 by an Eastern transplant, Maurice DeMond, whose passion for horses, big breakfasts, and good times quickly attracted L.A.'s leading business professional, social, and film elite. Long before golf and tennis became popular, horseback riding, polo, and showing in the forested oasis of Griffith Park was the favorite pastime of the City's civic movers and shakers.

Serving up a hearty outdoorsman's breakfast, Wild West tales, and the loan of a reliable mount to welcome the sunrise in the urban wilderness, DeMond's early morning gatherings turned into one of the city's most diverse and influential clubs. With its castle-like clubhouse in the park, it left a quixotic legacy where Will Rogers made President Calvin Coolidge laugh, where Jack Dempsey and Ed "Strangler" Lewis talked sports, and Irving Berlin crooned to one of his latest hits.

It's where Edgar Rice Burroughs and Michael Arlen talked about everything except books and authors. It's where rival newspaper tycoons William Randolph Hearst and Harry Chandler broke bread together. It's where cigar-chomping "speed king" Barney Oldfield shared the club's mascot—a wooden horse—with Dutch airplane designer Anthony Fokker.

The club's founding fathers drew from the ranks of the well-heeled, powerful, and famous—those who could afford not to be stuck behind their desks every Wednesday morning. Being an ambitious promoter, DeMond purchased five acres of a dairy farm at the entrance of Griffith Park with the members' entrance fees. He then enticed the colorful USC Chancellor, Rufus B. von Kleinsmid, to take over as president. Membership soon increased to one thousand, and entrance fees rose substantially.

With a fattened till, the club tore down the old farmhouse and built its first breakfast hall, the "Pavilion of Friendship," along with a riding ring with box seats for horse shows. Sitting at the outdoor horseshoe-shaped table in Friendship Garden, sharing a love of cowboy heroes, and indulging in jokes and a taste for ham and eggs, the trailblazers often listened to everything from singing cowboys to opera stars.

Enthusiastic club supporters Harry and Jack Warner donated ninety minutes on their radio station to broadcast the club's "Ham & Eggs" program. Despite the heckling of speakers over laughter and the clinking of utensils against water glasses, the radio program survived for more than twenty-six years.

The club's chaplain, a Baptist preacher with a taste for horseplay, often regaled clubbers with stories of when he had Jack Dempsey and Will Rogers in a Bible class. One day the Reverend announced he would begin teaching the Epistles next Sunday. He turned to Will and asked, "Do you know what the Epistles are?" Rogers replied, "You bet your life; they're the wives of the apostles." Turning on Dempsey, Will said, "You don't need to laugh, Jack. I'll bet you five dollars you can't say the Lord's Prayer." Dempsey said, "I'll bet I can." When Dempsey finished, Will handed him five bucks and said, "Jack, I really didn't think you could do it."

Rogers, in fact, did win a bet with another club member, getting the somber-looking Coolidge to crack a smile. "I'm sorry," Rogers said as he gripped the president's hand, "I didn't get your name."

The club endured the death of DeMond, bankruptcy, and the Depression. Upon reorganizing, membership slowly increased until clubbers were parking four-wheeled horsepower outside their new clubhouse along the banks of the Los Angeles River, a few blocks away and across the river from the original clubhouse.

A few decades later, after the freeway squeezed between the road and the river, the club moved back to its original site—now city-owned property. The membership razed the original clubhouse, erected a new ranch-style building, donated "Friendship Auditorium" to the city, and negotiated a fifty-year lease.

During my high school years we danced to the likes of Spade Cooley and Billy Mize, whose radio and TV shows emanated from there. The thundering hooves have disappeared along with the cowboys, horse trainers, and movie stars, but the Breakfast Club still serves up a down-home spirit. "The Shrine of Friendship," as the original motto over the door advertises, carries on with Breakfast Club descendants who preserve their founding riders' hodge-podge of fanciful, intellectual, outlandish, irreverent wit.

Remembering That First Horse

I'm sure everyone remembers his or her first horse. I remember mine, as well as the ones we have given to our children and grandchildren, and it's even more of a thrill to watch them receive theirs over the years.

We presented our youngest granddaughter (nearly nine years old) with her first horse last Christmas. She had been riding a friend's horse (Rowdy) for about a year, and had asked Santa for one of her own at every visit. We drove the hundred miles the day before Christmas to deliver the horse (a surprise) to the stable where she rode, and then proceeded to the house about a mile away. We had brought her a new halter on the pretext of using it on her borrowed mount. We visited for a while and then told her we needed to go to the barn to try the halter on Rowdy. If it didn't fit, I'd bring her another at our next visit, was the way it was explained.

We arrived at the barn and Kyndra, walking between Bram and me, headed for her friend's stall. About halfway there I told her I didn't think the halter would fit Rowdy, but I'd bet it would just fit her own horse. She promptly said to me, "But Granddaddy, I don't have a horse." Whereupon I said, pointing, "If the halter fits that horse over there, you do now."

"Whoaaa . . . !" She exclaimed, stopping dead in her tracks. When she realized I wasn't teasing, she bounded toward the new horse, halter in hand, and entered the corral. Her new chestnut Quarter Horse dropped his head right into the halter and gave her a nuzzle. We had brought along a saddle, which was a little big because it was the one her mother had ridden during her teenage years, but it was good enough for now. The smile has not been off

Kyndra's face since Christmas Eve, and I don't think she slept for the first few days.

During the holiday season, everyone talked about first horses and reminded us of how our other granddaughters had received theirs. I had been on a trip through Texas several years ago and came across the perfect horse for my wife. The only problem, which was not really a problem, was that the mare was in foal. I bought her anyway and had her shipped home with the idea we'd give the foal to our granddaughters.

We had a pasture that bordered the school bus stop where our granddaughters were deposited after school. Every day before going home, they'd stop and take from their lunch pails carrots, apples, or both, and the mare would meet them for goodies. This particular afternoon, she was lying down near the fence because it was foaling time. Our granddaughters watched in amazement, as did a telephone lineman on a pole some ten feet away. The phone man, being a city-raised person, had obviously been shaken after witnessing the miraculous birth of our first foal; he called into the office and had to request the rest of the day off.

In the meantime, our daughter had come to see why her girls were late getting home from school. When she saw the mare was down, she ran to our house to alert her mother. A little panic was evident, for my wife quickly tracked me down (I was at a meeting in town). It just so happened that attending the same meeting was our veterinarian, Dr. Willard Ommert. Out of breath, my wife said, "Honey, the mare's foaling! What should I do?" With that, I handed the phone to our vet. He listened for a moment and then said to her, "Can you boil some water?" "Yes," She said quickly. "Okay, do it," he replied. After a pause, she was back on the line and said, "Okay, the water's on." He then asked her if she had a little bourbon. Another pause. When she came back on the line, she assured him she had found some. "Okay," he said, "after the water is hot, put it in a large cup, pour in a little bourbon, sit down, and drink it. When you finish, everything will be done." There was dead silence on the phone, finally a chuckle, and a click. Foaling had always been my responsibility and our vet had just checked the mare, so I knew everything would be fine. By the time my wife got to the pasture, sure enough, our granddaughters' first horse was trying to wobble up on four legs. We promptly named her after both of them and still have the mare today.

As we kept reliving stories, they teased me about the time I sold Richard Widmark his first horse. His daughter was training with me at the time, and he wanted the right horse for a movie role. I just happened to have it. "Flashy, broke, plenty of handle, even might want to play a little polo," was the way it was put to me. He came out to look. I showed him the horse, rode it a little, and then decided polo would be great. (I had had a lot of experience stick-and-balling polo ponies right after I was discharged from the Navy.)

Dick, his wife, his daughter, and several other spectators were perched on the fence as I demonstrated my prowess, as well as the horse's. I swung the mallet like a pro (I thought) and while galloping around the arena, my confidence swelled with each phase. I galloped down the rail and decided to do an under-the-neck shot as a grand finale. I stood in my stirrups, leaned over, and swung the mallet under the horse's neck. To my surprise, the horse planted all four feet, stopping on the forehand, which sent me in a somersault, landing upside down, flat on my back, looking up directly into the face of my prospective buyer. He gave me the once-over and said, "Would you do that again? I'll go and get my camera." I think he bought the horse only to be able to reiterate the story over and over, which he did.

Revisiting a Friend's Oklahoma Roots

T he cattle were lowing as we drove down the long driveway to
the house. Ignoring the front door, I was ushered through the
back porch entrance (as one does when going home). The aroma of
coffee greeted us, which was a welcome from the chill outside.

"Don, I want you to meet Don," my host said, with a chuckle,
knowing the name was a common denominator among the three of
us. "And this is my Mom," he continued. Anyone would quickly see
the resemblance between AQHA's Director of Marketing, Don
Treadway, and his parents.

The smell of ham and eggs and the bustle in the kitchen
brought back old memories; even the iron skillet was a familiarity.
If I had closed my eyes, I'd have sworn I was back in the home of
my youth.

Always eager for new adventures, I had readily accepted the invitation to go with "Tread" for a day to his old stomping grounds a
couple of hours' drive from the World Showgrounds in Oklahoma
City. We could visit several historic sites around Pawhuska and
have a chance to meet with Ben Johnson's sister (who still lives on
a ranch close to where Ben had grown up). I remembered when
Ben had lived in a room in our barn for a while (after he first
came to Burbank with a load of horses), and even though I had
never met Ben's sister before, Tread thought we would have much
to talk about.

After I'd filled my belly with a real ranch breakfast, the senior
Mr. Treadway mapped out our plan, and luckily for us (as I found
out later), he was to be our guide.

We headed out cross-country toward Ben's sister's house. After several forks in the road, (turn here, veer off there, and no signs), we came to a three-way decision. Don's dad said, "I think we take the right-hand road." Tread differed, saying "No, I don't think so, we should go straight." "Son, I think we should turn right," the senior Don reiterated. We continued straight ahead until the senior Don finally broke the silence. "Think you've gone far enough, son?" Stopping the car, we waved down an oncoming local and asked directions. Seems we should have made a right turn back at the three-way. I just chuckled to myself, remembering my own folly of once getting lost in a trailer park.

Being a world champion at getting lost, I can sympathize with Don when people refer to him as the "lost Treadway." However, I've traveled with him before, and on every occasion we've gotten lost—sometimes for an instant, but more often than not it's been longer. This was one of the longer times. Like the Energizer Bunny, we kept going and going.

Back-tracking, we finally found the road to the house. Ben's sister was waiting and filled us with stories not only of the Ben I knew but also of his father, Ben Johnson, Sr., who was a legend in that area. Foreman of the famous Chapman Barnard ranch and an all-around cowboy, he was respected, even revered, by those who rode with him; they even dedicated a trail in his honor.

I couldn't wait to visit the historical site of the Barnard headquarters (which was, as it turned out, the last of the three forks). Tread, now heeding his dad's instructions to the letter, had no trouble hitting our target. We toured the headquarters and the museum that related the history of the ranch area and the famous people who had been part of its heritage.

We then routed the car along roads in Osage County that led to various towns and notable sites, such as the million-dollar elm tree where oil rights were auctioned off. We stopped at a local favorite, a barbecue place filled, as always, with those who knew great food. We were seated with others at a table, as was the custom. An empty chair was not only for eating but also for socializing. I was studying the menu when the waitress came; without hesitation, Don's dad ordered cowboy beans and cornbread. "Make that two," I chimed in, as I tripped down memory lane.

Our journey took us to other local ranches of note, one being the homestead of Don's friend, John Payne, who is also known as "the one-armed bandit." We chatted with cowboys out working and waved at longtime friends and neighbors. Finally returning to the boyhood home of my host, we said our goodbyes, and prodding ourselves, we got on the road back to the real world.

Along the way we stopped at the site of the famous 101 Ranch headquarters. As I walked around, I remembered those I knew as a boy who got their start at the 101 and went on to become movie stars.

That night, back at the Show, everyone asked what the day had been like. To me it was one I'll always remember—the countryside, the people, and the real pride I found in those who love the land.

I guess the other thing that stuck in my mind was when Don's dad taught me about the different kinds of grass that grow there. When we were at the Barnard Chapman ranch, they had a display of several types of grass that were native to the area. My botany lesson was to learn the differences. "Yes, I see the varieties—tall, short, broad, thin," I said, examining each kind. Then, from the man of deep conviction, came the real test. "You can't just see, you must feel . . . here, feel the grass." The senior Don took my hands and showed me how I could feel the difference just like the Indians did, and the cattle and buffalo as well.

Ever since then, I don't just look at the grass, I feel it. What a great lesson and a great day! Thanks, Tread . . .

Back in the Old Days

"**W**ho'd a thunk" that some fifty years ago I was just finishing boot camp, U.S. Navy style, in San Diego, California. Frequently when on "liberty," I'd hitch a ride to Mac's, a young horse trainer, artist, and family friend named Mac McHugh who lived in the area. As Fate smiled down, Mac was commissioned to draw the cover for the first Quarter Horse Journal. This rekindled Mac's enthusiasm for drawing and we both became excited about the new magazine. It was just prior to being assigned to active duty with Gene Autry's USO Tour (riding horses for Uncle Sam), that the Quarter Horse industry was moving into high gear. Mac received several advance copies of the new journal and I immediately "glommed" onto one, tucking it into my duffel bag, so I could be a hit when I went home on leave.

My dad's barn, which was really a riding academy, training, and sales yard called the Rocking Horse, was home to a multitude of horsemen, cowboys, actors, actresses, and "wannabes." We were just across the street from Ride-a-While Stables and Showgrounds, better known as Fickett's Corner, where most of the area's horse shows were held. On the other side of us was the Pickwick Stable and next to that was the Amble Inn, owned by champion cowboys Jerry Ambler and Bill and Bud Linderman. Not far away was another watering hole, the Painted Post Saloon, owned by cowboy movie star Hoot Gibson (who cowboyed for a living at one time).

Quarter Horses were becoming the horse of choice by most in the River Bottom of Burbank. In fact, the inspector for that region was a motion picture wrangler named John Lilly who later acquired a stallion called Honest John. When I arrived home on leave with the newly issued magazine, I wanted to show off that I had one of the first copies. By only walking a few yards, I was able to impress some of the greatest trainers of that era—M. R. Valdez, Jimmy Williams, Clyde Kennedy, Carl Helm, Pete Archibald, Whiskey Bill, Hutch Hutchison, and Mark Smith, to name a few. Not one to neglect the girls, I also shared the magazine with trick riders Donna Hall, Pat North, and Shirley and Sharon Lucas.

On a different note, one rather infamous name comes to mind—that of Red Foster. Because of being suspended from the AQHA, Red decided to compete and start up his own registry, The Model Quarter Horse Association. As I remember it, because we bought, sold, and traded a lot of horses, Red would come by the barn in his van, which contained a large rolltop desk housing all of his registry papers. Always touting his product, he'd say, "If you sign up with me, I'll make you a deal you can't refuse." How old do you want him and who do you want him by, was his pitch to register your horse.

There were some well-known horses at that time—Rango, shown by Clyde Kennedy; Champagne, with Jimmy Williams; and Ebony Night, with the great Valdez—all top stock horses, the forerunners to reining. The fastest horse then for 200 yards was Dog, a bulldoggin' Quarter Horse owned by Homer Dixon and ridden at times by me, while I was still in school. Rodeo cowboys Wag Blessing and "Hollywood Bob" Maynard (who wrangled some on the side) would continually argue over which horses were best.

The popularity of Steeldust horses (as many old-timers still called them then) was growing, along with the Hollywood star image. Fat Jones (Buck Jones's brother and Ben Johnson's father-in-law), Hudkins Bros., Meyers and Wills, Ralph McCutcheon, and Glenn Randall all furnished horses for the movies and featured Quarter Horses in their remudas. Local breeders were acquiring stallions at a fast pace. Ray Sence brought Ed Echols to the area, and for the next couple of years his program was the hot topic at the coffee shop.

The Los Angeles Horse and Mule Auction was going strong and any horse with papers, permanent or appendix, brought more money. While on leave, I even found time to ride a few through the sale. I'd hustle fifty cents a head, or a whole dollar if I did a hind crouper or somersault to show how gentle the horse was.

Having just reckoned with school reunion time, I've been reliving those carefree days of 1948—rodeoing and showing horses right up to cap and gown day; being afoot for a few weeks before my first liberty; being the first at home to sport the *Quarter Horse Journal*, whipping it out at every chance to brag about knowing the artist whose work emblazoned the cover. At that time I never dreamed that fifty years later I would be a literary contributor (because in school I "weren't" red hot with grammar and didn't spell "too good neither."). Thank goodness I married Ardy!

Don Quixote

Every once in a while when I kinda slacked off on my preparation, my dad used to say, "Son, you're getting a little too big for your britches." It took years for this to sink in and even now I discover I need to refresh my memory.

The latest reminder appeared on our monthly "things to do" agenda. Who was going to represent the AQHA in the sponsor's cutting at the National Cutting Horse Association's summer spectacular classic? Of the five executive Committee members, Rob Brown had the duty in Colorado, Mike Perkins was in Paraguay, Ginger Hyland had pressing business at home, and Ken Smith was in Wyoming. Guess whom that left? I really wanted to do it anyway, or at least it sounded great at the time, especially in conversation when people would ask what I was doing next. All my old armchair athlete cronies were green-eyed when I told them I was showing a cutting horse in Fort Worth.

A few months prior, the NCHA office wrote me for a bio, picture, and hat size—all of the goodies that go along with star status. If I had thought about it then, I'd have realized my britches were getting mighty snug. But I thought, this will be a piece of cake. Four or five wannabes would be strutting our stuff on Saturday night in front of the real cutters.

I was informed there would be a rider's clinic before the show. Great, I thought, a chance to polish my skills. I fully intended to ride my horse every day at home, but somehow the time just slipped by. Instead, the week before the event, I managed to ride my horse for two days. I spun, slid, galloped, and pretended for probably a half hour each day, thinking I was shaping up.

What's to worry, I thought; I was born in the saddle and can ride anything.

My mind, being that of a twenty-five-year-old, forgot that the seat of my pants was forty years older. I should have read the signs or omens. Two days before my wife and I were to depart, our airline tickets had not arrived. A call to our ever trustworthy travel agent assured me they had been sent Federal Express two days before. A little panic was setting in the afternoon of the day before we were to leave and no tickets yet. They finally arrived just hours before departure. "Not to worry," my always optimistic wife kept reassuring me.

Arriving at DFW, we were whisked to our hotel and then to the riders' dinner. My spirits dampened slightly when I found out there were sixteen riders, some of whom show all the time. They had brought their own horses, saddles, and trainers. I had my Sparks Rust spurs and well-worn chaps that have been let out in every seam. I had no idea who my trainer was nor what horse I was to ride until someone at our table said, "Oh, you've got one of the best trainers and he'll probably have you ride Widow-Maker." At the time, the name meant nothing to me.

After margaritas and enchiladas, all the riders were to pick one of the pinatas that decorated the room. When all sixteen pinatas had been chosen (we thought they were door prizes), the emcee told us to turn each one over and we would find a number tucked on the underside. It was to be our work order. I drew number thirteen. Some chuckled, some gave condolences. My wife congratulated me and said, "At least you don't have to go first."

We were to practice at three the next afternoon and show at seven that evening. So in the morning we headed for the arena to watch the other classes, find my appointed trainer, and check out my horse. Not knowing what my trainer looked like, we decided to head over to the practice arena. En route, we just happened to stumble upon a bulletin board displaying a program, write-up, and picture of my professional guide (a good sign). We got to the practice pen and quickly recognized my teacher who was schooling a horse. When he finished, I introduced myself. We talked and I had another panic attack; he thought the special sponsor cutting was the next day. My horse was at home, which was two hours away. "No problem," he said and hurried away to find someone to bring my mount by 3:00 P.M. It was now noon.

We returned for my lesson at 2:30 and found my pro schooling a big moving, quick athlete, doing things I've never seen a horse do. It was lesson time and I was first gunner. No warm-up, no lope, no trot, no nothing! I was to go in and cut a cow out with two hundred eyes watching me. I thought they'd at least let me ride around and get accustomed to the horse. What happened to the clinic? While this great horse ducked and dived, I not only perspired, I changed my lavender shirt to dark purple in a matter of seconds just trying to stay on. I was over-mounted to say the least, and after my five-minute session was over, never in my life have I felt so inadequate.

I went back to the hotel to rest and gather my thoughts, wondering what in the world I had gotten myself into. My wife, white as a sheet, assured me I didn't look that bad. I knew otherwise.

Seven o'clock did come and the first twelve cutters were scoring 210, 220, 223, etc. No one had fallen off yet; they were all good. I finally got to warm up, and my consummate professional trainer, Ascencion Banuelos, coached me every step of the way. During the warm-up, he crammed more cutting expertise into my head than I'll ever use in a lifetime. I slowly began to feel a diluted amount of confidence return to the pit of my stomach.

I was next. I raised my hand, passed the start marker, pulled my hat down and prayed. Everyone said I looked great, a real pro, and offered congratulations. I scored a 222, one point out of first place. You know, reserve champion isn't bad for a Don Quixote, impossible dreamer like me.

Just Call Me Rusty

You never know when you answer the phone who is going to greet you from the other end. After my hello, an unfamiliar voice said, "Is this Rusty?" "No," I answered, "there's no one named Rusty here." The voice then asked, "Is this Don Burt?" I said, "Yes." The voice continued, "Well, didn't you used to be Rusty?"

I was dumbfounded. About forty-plus years ago, I did go through a phase when I didn't like my name. In fact, Don Dodge and I reminisced about that not long ago. In my younger days, I thought I needed something more theatrical, a name with more pizzazz. At the time, I was doing a TV show with my trick horse and showing on the side, and I needed a change. So I told everybody, "Just call me Rusty."

I thought it sounded great until one day at a show, sitting on a tack trunk with Mr. Dodge, I asked for his opinion. He said to me, "I believe in keeping things short and simple—make them mean something—and that particularly applies to your name." I have always remembered those words of wisdom, which put an abrupt end to Rusty.

This voice from my past evidently knew me in my Rusty days, as he went on to say, "That trick horse of yours sure had a mind of his own. I don't know if you remember, but I was the vet you called when he went lame on the show." We talked and shared the memories of my alias and that particular TV episode with Frosty, the wonder horse.

In those days, all the shows were done "live," no retakes. We would rehearse all week to ensure that the hour-long show would air without a hitch. The day of the show, we arrived late at the barn only to find Frosty was not in his stall. Glancing around, we discovered the other horses were not in their stalls either—Frosty had let them all out! Someone had forgotten to put the snap lock on his latch. Spotting the silhouettes grazing in the distance, we started the "dawn patrol" roundup.

With the clock ticking, we arrived on the set with only fifteen minutes to spare before airtime. I hurriedly unloaded Frosty only to find him limping as he came out of the trailer. "Oh, no! He's lame," I said. Picking up his left front foot, I found a small rusty nail buried about halfway in the frog. We definitely couldn't do a dance act with a lame horse on "live" television.

"Come on you guys," the director yelled, "you're on in five minutes and you're not even in costume yet." "I'm not worried about the costumes," I said. "Frosty can't walk." The director gasped, "He can't what?" Reiterating, I said, "He's lame."

About that time my brain took over and I came up with a solution: "Let's do the whole episode around Frosty being hurt. We'll call the vet and have him treat Frosty right on television. By the end of the episode we can show his complete recovery!"

Just as we got the horse into position, the red light on the camera came on and we were standing there being watched by thousands of viewers. It was quite an opening scene. There was a crowd around Frosty with no one in costume or makeup (someone did have the presence of mind to put on Frosty's mask, which gave him magical powers). Since we had not rehearsed, we had to ad lib.

I started off by talking about safety, the do's and don'ts of going barefoot, not watching where you are going—and, at the same time, casting a side glance or two at Frosty. I told our viewers why Frosty was hurt and brought out a phone to actually call the veterinarian from the set. I asked Frosty if *he* wanted to tell the vet what happened, but he shook his head "no." I then asked if he wanted *me* to tell the vet and he shook his head "yes."

The veterinarian arrived, examined the foot, and made his diagnosis. First, he removed the nail and we made quite a production out of giving Frosty the tetanus shot. Then we got a rubber bucket, filled it with hot water and Epsom salts, and stuck Frosty's foot in it.

We went through our normal routine of having Frosty read the funny papers, do some more "yes" and "no" tricks, and play the games with the kids in the audience. Frosty did not enter into these games as he usually did; he just stood there throughout the show very content with his foot in the bucket. Several times the vet would check his pulse and the water temperature to make sure Frosty was comfortable.

As the show drew to a close, it was time to prove that Frosty was all right. The vet came to lift his foot out of the bucket but Frosty's foot was steadfast. He refused to budge. Not being an actor, the vet was somewhat embarrassed at not being able to pick up Frosty's foot. He called me and I tried . . . no luck. We both pulled and tugged but Frosty just put more weight on his foot. Other people came to our rescue, but to no avail.

We went off the air like a Keystone Cops Comedy, the smug horse just standing there with his foot in a bucket while six people fell all over themselves trying to pull it out. When the red light went off on the camera, Frosty simply raised his foot and walked off the set.

The veterinarian had often told this story to his grandkids, and it seems that over the years, he had been asking people if they knew a Rusty Burt. Of course, no one did. We had a great visit.

Later that day, my wife and I went to a surprise seventieth birthday party for a friend. There were several guests there whom I didn't know, so when the introductions started, Ardy said, "Oh, just call him Rusty!"

Knowledge Gained
Should Be Shared

U p at 5:00 A.M., on horseback by 5:30 to watch the sun rise, I loped up to what my kids call "Dad's plottin' place." It's a bluff where the salt air saddles the sea gulls on their morning hunt and herds of whitecaps graze across the ocean. In the distance the spout of a whale returning from its southern migration can be seen, and the sound of waves connecting with the shore is all that breaks the silence.

It was twenty-two years ago I'm referring to, when, as Frosty nibbled the grass, I made notes on my pad and "Horsing Around" was born. It started with thoughts my dad instilled in me through the years. "Knowledge gained should be shared," he believed, and "the experiences of one should soon find a home with others through communication."

Since then, I've visited with great horsemen in nearly every country, and swapped tales and trade secrets with them. Having judged over a thousand shows and too many horses even to try to count, I look back at some of the words I've written and thoughts I've passed on. Whether you've just gotten into the horse world or have been around as long as I have, there will always be clues to make you think and hopefully become better horsemen.

Some advice remains constant over the years, such as "think soft" and "prepare the mind." These are terms often used when horse training is discussed. With our schooling ideas becoming more sophisticated, the need arises to communicate these ideas to others. The trainers who have been doing things "by the seat of their pants" must now be able to describe what is taking place.

While horsemen, since time began, have subconsciously worked on the mind of the horse, it is now a necessity to be able to peak the show horse, let him down, and peak him again just at the right moment. We put a great deal more strain on the horse physically with today's demands. This should lead to an increased sensitivity on the trainer's part where the horse's mind is concerned. There must be a time to relax, a time to soften, and it must be taught at the very beginning.

Basics are the key to future success in any horse's curriculum. The often-tried gimmicks will continue to be used, I'm sure, but basic conditioning, both physical and mental, ultimately equips a horse for any task.

While visiting with a well-known, successful trainer the other day, I asked him if he would have changed anything along the way. "Well, Don," he said, "I've made and ruined hundreds of horses over the years, but I wouldn't have done anything else but train horses, if that's what you mean. Only thing is, I wouldn't have started until I was fifty, because that's when I finally got smart and began to think like a horse." I chuckled and the following discussion came to pass:

"I decided to ask and not tell," were his words, "to allow the horse the opportunity to learn instead of beating it into him by demanding perfection at every phase. Each horse is different, you know; some learn rapidly while others—just like people—are slower. So, I do exercises to find out how fast each horse will arrive at a certain point. I plan ahead; then I know how to set up a training schedule for that individual.

"First, I look 'em over while they're standing still to see if the horse has correct angulation. Every event requires just a little difference in conformation, so I kinda analyze what category I think a particular horse would fit into. Then I move them on the line, trot 'em out or watch 'em move in a pen. I study the action or what the horse does naturally; high or low action, high or low head carriage. Then the next step is to find out what the horse wants to be, keeping in mind the category I've selected for him.

"Through the entire training routine, I work on the mind; keep the horse thinking, soft and willing. I never hurt him or take him beyond his mental capacity to learn a given thing.

"What tells me a lot about a horse is his ability to take collection, so this is where I begin. Snaffle and running martingale are the tools I start with; handle 'em with both hands, start slow, and don't ask for much. As the training progresses, keep up the impulsion and allow the horse to use the bridle as a barrier he can't go beyond. Let him collect for a time, then relax, soften, collect again, relax, and soften; the horse will tell you. When he softens or drops off, then you relax and let the horse be steady.

"When he can be collected for a period of time—depending on the amount of impulsion—and be happy, he'll tell you what he wants to be. He'll find that spot where collection is comfortable and impulsion allows him to balance. Then I look at the action and where he wants to carry his head. Through this period I work the horse often, but just a little while at a time. A tired or irritated horse won't learn anything. A horse's mind can absorb only so much, so don't demand more.

"Horses, for the most part, don't think like humans or other animals, but they have a capacity for association, an inherent instinct, and that's the part of the mind I work on. Keep 'em comfortable, happy, and eager for the next lesson.

"Even I get tired of the same old thing, so I insert arcs and flexions to keep the horse's mind from going stale. From arcs and flexions and lots of circling, I go into two-tracking to control the horse's body, and teach him to move away from the leg, which is also what we did with circles and arcs. Handle him a lot, take and relax, teach and soften, allow the horse a time to escape.

"People tend to become 'pickers' when schooling the mind. They jerk or spur every time a horse makes a little mistake; some pick at the horse constantly. When we relax, we should drop everything, take away all pressures, reins and legs, and let him down. Cultivate his intellect, don't agitate him into submission. Some horses require more firmness than others and have to be gotten after sometimes to keep their attention. Changing places or surroundings, gaits, and transitions, along with complete abandon or release, makes the horse work and relax on cue.

"Be satisfied with a little progress each time and don't expect miracles. If the horse gives to you once or twice at the outset, accept it. Never punish a horse for what he doesn't understand; horses do associate punishment with situations or surroundings."

Our discussion ended and I reflected on my initial question about change. Twenty-two years have passed and here I am at the same spot, with the same surroundings and feelings, only riding a different horse. The horse business has changed, though, and will continue to do so. In April of 1973, I wrote "The ABC's of Winning" (still timely today). In that text, "X" was for xenophobia, which means fear of anything foreign or strange. To be a winner, you must accept change; and don't hesitate to try something new if you've thought it all out before. To quote the old saying, "The turtle never goes anywhere until he sticks his neck out."

However, the areas that never change include the quality of life with horses, each individual's interpretation and use of the written word, and the intimacy of experiences shared. Hasta luego, amigos.